100 BOOKS

THAT SHAPED WORLD HISTORY

Miriam Raftery

A Bluewood Book

This edition produced and published
by Bluewood Books
A Division of The Siyeh Group, Inc.,
P.O. Box 689
San Mateo, CA 94401

ISBN 0-912517-48-4

Printed in U.S.A.
10, 9, 8, 7, 6, 5, 4, 3, 2, 1

Editor: Tony Napoli
Designer: Kevin Harris

Key to cover illustration:
Clockwise, starting from top left:
Hippocrates, Albert Einstein,
Andreas Vesalius, Mark Twain,
Charles Dickens, Anne Frank, and
Confucius in the center.

About the Author:
Miriam Raftery is a Southern
California based freelance writer. She
is the author of Apollo's Fault (1996),
and has written numerous nonfiction
articles for regional and national pub-
lications. Ms. Raftery has won "Best
Historical Article" from the National
Federation of Press Women and "Best
News and Feature Article" from the
California Press Women.

Picture Acknowledgements:
All images and photos from Bluewood
Archives; Library of Congress;
National Archives; National Portrait
Gallery; San Mateo Library; and the
White House with the following excep-
tions: Ballentine Books: 81; Bantam
Books: 70; Tony Chikes: 58, 73, 75,
85, 107; Farrar, Strauss & Giroux:
107; Grosset & Dunlap: 65, 71;
HarperCollins Publishers: 96; Harper
& Row Publishers: 103, 105; Holt,
Rinehart and Winston: 104; Little,
Brown and Company: 94; Coward S.
McCann & Geoghegan, Inc.: 95;
McGraw-Hill Book Co.: 100;
Nebraska State Historical Society: 72;
Oxford University Press: 80; Charles
Scribner's Sons: 92; Simon and
Schuster: 97; and Vintage Books: 83.

TABLE OF CONTENTS

1. 2.   3. 4.5.   6.7. 8. 9.10.   11.12.13.14. 16. 23.
17. |24.
18. 25.
15.   19.
20.   26.
21.
22.

2700 B.C.   **A.D. 1700**

TABLE OF CONTENTS

27.   28.   29.   30.   32.   34.   36.   37.   38.   39.   40   41.   42.   43.   44.   45.   46.   47.   48.
33.   35.

1701   **1865**

TABLE OF CONTENTS

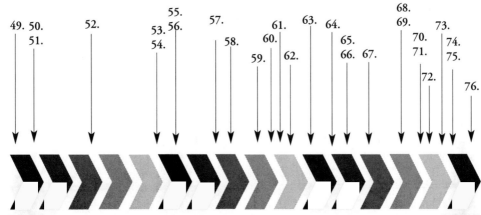

1866   1930

TABLE OF CONTENTS

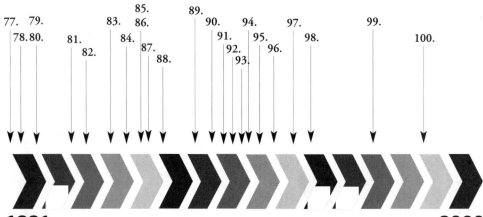

1931　　　　　　　　　　　　　　　　　　　2000

INTRODUCTION

Choosing a list of 100 books that shaped world history has been a challenging and fascinating experience—and one made even more difficult if you first begin by trying to define the word "book."

The word book evokes images of a bound volume containing pages made of paper. However, before civilization developed a written alphabet, stories were passed down by oral tradition. Some were not written down until hundreds or even thousands of years later, making precise dating difficult.

Early books bear little resemblance to modern-day volumes. At first, symbols were etched on stone tablets. Ancient Egyptians used papyrus scrolls, or wrote on pyramid walls. Later innovations, such as paper and ink, enabled more people to become writers. The world's population remained largely illiterate, however, since few people could afford rare and costly hand-copied manuscripts.

The number of books increased dramatically with technological advances. Gutenberg's printing press in 1455 made books widely available, rapidly improving literacy rates. Typewriters, introduced in 1843, increased authors' output; more books were printed in the late 1900s than in the entire previous history of mankind.

By the late 20th century, computers made writing and editing books faster and easier than ever before. The high percentage of 19th and 20th century works chosen for this list reflects the amazing increase in book publishing over the past 200 years.

As for what titles we have chosen, we have tried to present a cross-section—from ancient times to modern, from different corners of the world, by both male and female writers. Our criteria was not limited to those works that were only published in book form. We selected written works, in whatever form they originally took, which significantly shaped history.

Some widely-read works triggered major historical events. For example, Martin Luther's *Ninety-Five Theses*—a proclamation nailed to a church door—caused an enormous split within the Catholic Church and started the Protestant Reformation. Thomas Paine's *Common Sense*—which has alternately been termed a book, booklet, or pamphlet—is credited with instigating the American colonists to begin their fight for independence. Harriet Beecher Stowe's *Uncle Tom's Cabin* sparked antislavery sentiments and helped ignite America's Civil War.

Some books shaped history beyond their own time. Henry David Thoreau's *Civil Disobedience*, written in 1848, profoundly influenced Mohandas Gandhi and Dr. Martin Luther King to practice passive resistance to unjust laws in the 20th century. Fifty years after Theodor Herzl strongly advocated a Jewish homeland in Palestine in his work *The Jewish State*, the nation of Israel was born.

Other books shaped history more subtly, altering readers' perceptions of themselves or their world. Aristotle and Plato introduced philosophy and classical wisdom. Copernicus and Einstein changed our perceptions of the universe. Darwin questioned the origin of mankind; Freud unlocked secrets of the unconscious mind.

Not every book shaped history in a positive way. The impact of such notorious works as Adolf Hitler's *Mein Kampf* cannot be overlooked, however.

Many of the titles we have chosen influenced the history of literature. Novels by such authors as Cervantes, Dickens, Brönte, Melville, Dostoevsky, Twain, Joyce, and Hemingway profoundly affected the literary styles of writers well beyond the times in which those books were published.

We have confined our selections to nonfiction and fiction prose, omitting books of poetry, plays, and reference works—with two exceptions. It seemed impossible to compile a list of 100 significant written works without including at least one by the person many people consider the world's greatest writer; so William Shakespeare is represented by his classic tragedy, *Romeo and Juliet*. In addition, we have listed perhaps the world's most comprehensive English-language reference book, the *Oxford English Dictionary*.

As we move into the early years of the 21st century, we wonder what will be the next book to shape history. Who knows—perhaps one written by a reader of this book, inspired by the creative works and authors described within these pages.

1. Epic of Gilgamesh
(c. 2700-1500 B.C.)

Born in the cradle of civilization more than 4,000 years ago, the *Epic of Gilgamesh* is among the world's oldest written works. A folk epic, not attributed to a single author, it was compiled from oral narratives and written texts created over more than a thousand-year span.

The epic weaves together stories and myths about **Gilgamesh**, an ancient king of **Babylonia**. Gilgamesh reigned in approximately 2700 B.C. along the Euphrates River in the region of present-day Iraq.

The first oral narratives arose at the time of Gilgamesh's reign. Tales of Gilgamesh were inscribed on clay tablets in the **Sumerian** language by 2000 B.C. Later, the stories were combined with tales from other languages in a long narrative written in a script known as cuneiform.

The *Epic of Gilgamesh* recounts the odyssey of a king who did not want to die. This enduring literary classic opens with the following introduction to its protagonist:

"I will proclaim to the world the deeds of Gilgamesh. This was the man to whom all things were known; this was the king who knew the countries of the world. He was wise, he saw mysteries and knew secret things, he brought us a tale of the days before the flood. He went on a long journey, was weary, worn-out with labor, returning he rested, he engraved on a stone the whole story."

The king, portrayed as half-man, half-god, embarks on a journey to seek eternal life.

Cuneiform writing on a clay tablet

Gilgamesh crosses into the underworld, where he must meet challenges to attain an elixir of immortality. When a serpent steals the elixir, Gilgamesh must return empty-handed to his people.

The experience, however, transforms Gilgamesh from a tyrant into a wise and good king. He builds walls to protect his kingdom from attacks, and brings civilization to his people. Thus the true benefit of his ordeal proves to be not discovering the secret of eternal life, but finding the secret of becoming a just and benevolent ruler.

The *Epic of Gilgamesh* remained unknown to the Western world until 1872, when archaeologists discovered stone tablets written in **Akkadian**, the language of the ancient Babylonians. The discovery created much excitement, because the tablets described a great flood. Many believed that this confirmed the Bible's account of the flood survived by Noah. Scholars now know that the Babylonian flood legend is much older, though some believe it may have been the source of the flood story told in Genesis.

The *Epic of Gilgamesh* was published in 1891 and 1930. Later, more tablets containing Gilgamesh stories were discovered. In 1985, scholar **Andrew George** began research to compile a new edition to include the newly discovered material; his comprehensive translation was published in 1999.

2. The Egyptian Book of the Dead
(c. 2400-1420 B.C.)

The Egyptian Book of the Dead served as one of the world's most important religious text for nearly 3,000 years. Although the concept that the dead must make a journey to an "other world" is found in many religions, *The Egyptian Book of the Dead* contains the earliest written expression of that concept.

The text detailed rituals to be performed for the dead, including spells, magic formulas, prayers, and incantations. These rituals were designed to assure passage of departed sprits into the Land of the Gods by transforming the deceased into mythological creatures.

The text also described mummification procedures, leading to remarkable preservation of ancient Egyptian culture. If those procedures had not been diligently followed, many of the greatest archaeological discoveries in modern times might never have occurred.

Numerous authors and compilers contributed to *The Egyptian Book of the Dead*. Early chapters were carved on pyramid walls around 2400 B.C. Other texts were painted on mummy cases or written on papyrus scrolls. Coffin texts date from 2000 B.C.; painted text on mummy cases continued into the Christian Era.

Later, scribes copied the sacred texts onto papyrus scrolls, which often included colorful illustrations. The papyrus texts were sold to important individuals, who saved them for use in burials of themselves or family members. Texts were read aloud at funerals; rituals were closely followed to assure immortality of the deceased.

The Egyptian Book of the Dead opens with a prayer to **Osiris**, an Egyptian god.

"Homage to thee, Osiris, Lord of eternity, King of the Gods."

Subsequent sections recount mystical ceremonies, such as the lighting of four torches of atma cloth anointed with unguent to assure immortality.

"They shall burn the torches in the beautiful light of **Ra** (Egyptian god of the sun), and this shall confer power and might upon the Spirit-soul of the deceased among the stars which never set. If this Chapter be recited for him he shall never, never perish, and he shall become a living soul for ever."

Partial copies of the book have been discovered by archaeologists inside Egyptian tombs. In 1842, German Egyptologist **Karl Richard Lepsius** published the first collection of the texts, which were literally titled *The Chapters of Coming-Forth-by-Day*.

The most comprehensive collection of texts was composed around 1420 B.C. by **Ani**, a scribe and bookkeeper of the Pharoah's grain silos. Ani's papyrus scrolls were obtained by **E.A. Wallis Budge**, curator of the British Museum's Egyptian Antiquities, in the late 19th century. Budge, a famed Egyptologist, published a translation of the scrolls, which became among the museum's greatest treasures.

Fragment from *The Egyptian Book of the Dead*

9

3. Iliad
(c. 800 B.C.) Homer

The *Iliad* and its sequel, the *Odyssey*, epic poems of ancient **Greece,** rank among the world's most influential works of literature.

An epic poem recounts events proclaimed to be true, often derived from legends, myths, or religions of a civilization. The epic hero follows a code of honor, and is willing to make great personal sacrifices, yet also possesses tragic mortal flaws.

The *Iliad* commemorates heroic deeds of ancient **Achaean** warriors during the **Trojan War**. In addition, the *Iliad* provides moral, theological, and practical instructions that have endured through the ages.

The *Iliad* and the *Odyssey* formed the basis of classical Greek education. They remained important cultural elements until the rise of the Roman Empire and the spread of Christianity. **Alexander the Great** used the *Iliad* as a manual on warfare. The *Iliad* was also the predominant influence on **Herodutus,** the world's first historian.

Little is known of **Homer,** the poet credited with creating both epics. Some historians have questioned whether Homer actually existed, believing the poems may have been written by several contributors rather than a single author.

The *Iliad* recounts events which took place in the 12th century B.C. For many years, it was believed that Homer lived during that time period. Archaeological discoveries in the early 20th century, however, indicate that Homer probably lived during the 9th century B.C. Relying upon oral accounts passed down through many generations, Homer apparently wrote the epic poems about 400 years after the events described had occurred.

The *Iliad* opens during the siege of Troy, nine years after the conflict began. The Achaeans are determined to see Troy fall in order to retrieve Helen, wife of the Achaean king's brother. Helen has been kidnapped by a Trojan prince.

The *Iliad's* hero, **Achilles**, prince of the Achaeans, suffers a tragic flaw: pride. His pride wounded, Achilles isolates himself aboard his ship. He refuses to fight with the Achaeans against the Trojans. Instead, he allows his best friend, Patroclus, to enter the battle. Devastated when Patroclus is killed by Hector of Troy, Achilles rejoins the fighting to regain his honor and take revenge.

A prophesy has warned that Achilles will die soon after Hector. Aware of the prophecy, Achilles slays Hector in battle, willing to accept his fate. The Trojan king pleads with Achilles to release his son's body, and returns to Troy with his dead son amid great mourning.

The book ends without disclosing the fates of Achilles or Troy. The story continues in the *Odyssey*, which recounts Ulysses' epic journey home from the Trojan War.

The *Iliad* and the *Odyssey* have profoundly influenced culture and literature throughout the world for thousands of years.

A bust of Homer

4. Aesop's Fables
(c. 600-560 B.C.) Aesop

Aesop's Fables is the world's most widely read book, with the exception of the Holy Scriptures. These simple morality tales have been translated into many languages and read in countries throughout the world.

Some scholars believe Aesop was a mythical figure, since certain fables attributed to him were actually written by others long after Aesop's supposed death. However, most historians believe Aesop was a slave born in ancient **Greece** around 620 B.C.

According to legend, Aesop's talent for telling fables earned him his freedom. As a freedman, Aesop traveled widely, speaking and teaching in many lands. King **Croesus of Lydia** hired Aesop as a diplomat. He asked Aesop to help establish peace among the Greek republics by telling the people wise fables.

On a mission to **Delphi**, Aesop brought gold to distribute. Upset by the citizens' greed, he returned the gold to the king. Enraged citizens executed Aesop by pushing him off a cliff.

Delphi later suffered disasters viewed as retribution for Aesop's death. The phrase, "the blood of Aesop" came into usage, carrying a moral of its own: wrongful deeds will not go unpunished.

Aesop's fables were passed down orally for centuries. The first known written collection of them was made in 300 B.C. by a Greek philosopher. Later, fables were translated into Latin and taught to Roman scholars.

Aesop telling a fable

The fables were forgotten for hundreds of years, until a 14th century monk in the Byzantine Empire made a collection. After the fall of Constantinople, fables were reintroduced in Italy. In 1610, Swiss scholar **Isaac Nicholas Nevelet** created a printed edition. His book became one of the most widely distributed volumes around the world.

Most of the fables are simple stories involving animals. Yet each also conveys deeper meaning, inviting listeners—or readers—to draw a moral conclusion.

"The Hare and the Tortoise," describes a race between the two animals. Confident that he cannot lose, the hare pauses to nap. Awakening, the hare finds that the plodding tortoise has crossed the finish line. Moral: slow and steady wins the race.

Aesop's Fables appealed to rulers as well as to common men. In "Androcles," an escaped slave pulls a thorn from a lion's paw. After the slave and lion are captured, Androcles is thrown to the hungry lion. The emperor is amazed when the lion licks Androcles' hand.

"The emperor, surprised at this, summoned Androcles to him, who told him the whole story. Whereupon the slave was pardoned and freed, and the lion let loose to his native forest."

Moral: gratitude is the sign of noble souls.

Many morals from *Aesop's Fables* have become household sayings, owing to their universal appeal.

The *Hippocratic Corpus* is a collection of approximately 50 medical treatises attributed to **Hippocrates**, the Greek physician known as the "**Father of Medicine.**"

Hippocrates founded a medical school on the Greek island of **Cos** sometime during the 5th century B.C. Before Hippocrates, the ancient Greeks believed that diseases and illnesses were caused by malevolent gods—and that cures could only be attained by appeasing those deities.

Hippocrates, by contrast, believed diseases had natural causes, which could be cured by rational methods. "Find the cause," he said, "then you can cure the disease." He was the first to establish medicine as a scientific discipline, rather than a religious one. His followers scorned remedies based on irrational beliefs.

In his written works, Hippocrates advised physicians on how to examine patients for symptoms, how to treat ailments, and

Hippocrates

how to record their observations. He urged physicians to use simple remedies, such as healthy diet, plenty of rest, and clean surroundings. He wrote, "Nature often brings a cure when doctors cannot."

The most notable follower of Hippocrates was **Galen**, a Greek doctor appointed to serve as physician at a gladiator school in the 2nd century A.D. Galen studied Hippocrates' works, making his own observations on anatomy, physiology, and surgeries. It was Galen who discovered that blood circulates in the body, that severing the spinal cord causes paralysis, and that a tracheotomy can save a patient with breathing problems.

Galen's ideas and observations, based on the Hippocratic methods, dominated medicine through the Middle Ages. His books were used in schools to train physicians.

Some of Hippocrates' theories were inaccurate. For example, he believed that illness could be caused by an imbalance among four "humours" of the body: black bile, yellow bile, phlegm, and blood. That belief has since been proven false.

Perhaps Hippocrates' most important contribution to modern medicine was his insistence that physicians should serve their patients, follow honorable standards of conduct, and adhere to a strict ethical code.

Hippocrates endorsed a pledge that is still affirmed today by medical students when they enter the profession. They swear to abide by the **Hippocratic Oath**, which states in part, "I solemnly pledge myself to consecrate my life to the service of humanity; I will practice my profession with conscience and dignity and the health of my patient will be my first consideration."

Thessalus, son of Hippocrates, may have published some works by his father, who scrawled on wax tablets and animal skins. Students of Hippocrates also recorded his teachings. They collected notes of his lectures and published books describing them, enabling future generations of physicians to benefit from his insights and wisdom.

6. The History of Herodotus

(c. 440 B.C.) Herodotus

The History of Herodotus—a history of the Greek and Persian wars written by the Greek historian **Herodotus**—is the first great narrative history produced in the ancient world.

Considered the father of modern historiography—the body of historical writing and thought—Herodotus lived in Turkey during the fifth century B.C. After he was exiled for reportedly conspiring against Persian rule, he spent many years traveling throughout the Mediterranean region, recording his well-researched observations about the places, people, and cultures he encountered on his journeys.

During the last years of his life, he wrote his narrative of the **Greco-Persian Wars**, which spanned the years 499-479 B.C. Herodotus wanted to record the momentous events he observed for posterity, as the opening of *The History of Herodotus* relates:

"These are the researches of Herodotus of Halicarnassus, which he publishes, in the hope of thereby preserving from decay the remembrances of what men have done, and of preventing the great and wonderful actions of the Greeks and the Barbarians from losing their due meed of glory; and withal to put on record what were their grounds of feuds."

Like Homer (see no. 3), Herodotus shared a gift for narrating history in a storyteller's entertaining style. Unlike Homer or other predecessors, however, Herodotus emphasized the actions and characters of actual persons—not the divine intervention of gods. This rationalistic approach was a dramatic innovation in the portrayal of historical events. Herodotus set another precedent by weaving dialogue, including speeches by historical leaders, into his descriptions and analysis of warfare and politics.

Herodotus described the background leading up to the Greco-Persian Wars, including the political situations of the many Greek city-states that would become embroiled in the

Herodotus reading to the Greeks

conflict. Later, he recounts the growth of the **Persian Empire**, its invasion of Greece, and the ensuing Greek victory.

Herodotus exhibited an objectivity unusual for his day, demonstrating no bias toward either the Greek or Persian viewpoint. However, Herodotus did extract a moral from his story of the Greco-Persian Wars, the greatest historical event of his time. In his narrative, he reveals his belief that prosperity is a "slippery thing" which can lead to a fall—especially when accompanied by arrogance and folly, as in the case of the Persian leader, **Xerxes**.

At the same time, Herodotus also recognized that the Greek victory, though glorious, had a dark side. He understood that the rise of **Athens** led to rivalry with **Sparta**, spurring disputes which later culminated in the disastrous Peloponnesian War (431-404 B.C.).

The historical narrative, practices introduced by Herodotus in his writings, strongly influenced future historians and writers for thousands of years to come.

7. The Analects of Confucius
(429 B.C.) Confucius

The Analects of Confucius, the written records of the teachings of the noted **Chinese** philosopher, have influenced both Western and Asian thought and culture for thousands of years.

Confucius (the Latinized form of the name **Kung-Fu-tzu**) was born around 551 B.C.. As a young man, he developed a love of learning, and sought out masters to teach him the six arts: ritual, music, archery, charioteering, calligraphy, and arithmetic.

His knowledge of history and poetry enabled him to begin a teaching career. He later served as a magistrate and minister of justice under Emperor Lu. Disillusioned because the emperor's inner circle had no interest in his ideas, Confucius left the country, but continued teaching loyal followers. In his sixties, he returned home and resumed teaching, writing down legends and stories to pass on to future generations. He died in 479 B.C.

Confucius

Fifty years later, the second generation of his followers compiled oral and written records of the master's sayings in *The Analects of Confucius. The Analects* consisted of poems, stories, and legends that Confucius had collected, as well as dialogues between the master and his disciples.

Confucius advocated an ethic known as **Jen**, translated as "love," "goodness," or "humanity." *The Analects* included this close parallel of the Biblical golden rule:

"Do not do unto others what you would not want others to do unto you."

Confucius also believed strongly in **filial piety**, or reverence to one's elders and family, believing that respect for family formed the basis for a good life. He urged rulers to set good examples through benevolent, honorable actions and taught subjects to be obedient to their sovereign.

Confucius's beliefs fell into disfavor in the centuries after his death. Copies of his work were destroyed, but others survived into the **Han Dynasty** (206-220 B.C.), when Confucianism became the dominant school of thought.

His ideas had a profound influence on Chinese social values and politics, later spreading to other Asian lands. His philosophy was intended to help individuals improve moral conduct, attain family harmony, and bring peace to the empire.

The Analects were edited into final form around A.D. 100, after the Chinese invented paper-making. In time, the book was discovered by Europeans, who published it under the Latinized version of the name Kung Fu-tzu.

Eventually, Confucianism in China was eclipsed by the rise of Taoism and Buddhism. While Confucius taught the importance of self-discovery, Buddhism stressed that to attain nirvana, or paradise, one must forget oneself and serve others. Later, Neo-Confucianism combined Confucian thought with Buddhist and Taoist philosophies.

Confucianism is practiced today as both a philosophy and a religion by several million people, mostly in Asia.

8. Republic
(c. 378 B.C.) Plato

In *Republic*, the **Greek** philosopher **Plato** presented his utopian vision of government, one founded on conceptions of law and justice. His views have influenced the founders of democratic governments around the world for more than two thousand years.

Born in Athens around 428 B.C., Plato was a student of Socrates, the famous philosopher and teacher. In 399 B.C., Socrates was charged with corrupting the youth of Athens, and bringing new religious practices into the city. He was condemned to death by the Athenian government; he drank poison after refusing a chance to escape and go into exile.

Horrified by the fate of his mentor, and disillusioned by democracy, Plato spent 12 years traveling and studying with major philosophers. He began writing philosophical dialogues similar in style to plays, often featuring conversations between Socrates and others.

In *Republic,* Plato presented an idealized structure of society in which three classes contribute to the community. He believed society should be ruled by just "guardians" distinguished by their abilities to grasp the truth of forms. Rulers would be defended by "auxiliaries," while "producers" would grow food and produce goods.

Like Socrates, Plato believed that heads of governments should be "**philosopher-kings**." Plato believed that concepts, such as justice, as well as objects, exist first as forms, and that morality and the good life, which the state should promote, are reflections of those ideal forms.

Plato used the simile of a cave to illustrate the point. Men, chained facing the cave wall with their backs to the light, see only shadows of reality and must be forced to face what is truly real. Similarly, Plato maintained, only philosopher-statesmen could comprehend the reality of forms and "face the brightest blaze of being" outside the metaphorical cave to become just leaders:

"Unless philosophers bear kingly rule in cities or those who are now called kings and princes become genuine and adequate philosophers, and political power and philosophy are brought together . . . there will be no respite from evil for cities."

Plato used dialogues with Socrates to challenge readers to examine the nature of goodness and justice. For example, Socrates ponders, if a person obtained a legendary ring which could magically make its wearer invisible, would that person still have reason to behave justly? Justice, Plato concluded, consists of harmony between the intellect, emotion, and desire.

Some have criticized Plato's views on society as narrow, promoting rigid class structure and elitism. Although his utopian vision of a society ruled by philosopher-kings may have been unrealistic, his belief that justice and happiness are inextricably linked has sparked ethical, political, and philosophical debates through the ages.

Socrates teaching Plato

9. Nicomachean Ethics
(c. 330 B.C.)   Aristotle

The *Nicomachean Ethics* ranks as one of the most significant works of **Aristotle**, the brilliant ancient **Greek** philosopher.

Born in Macedonia in 384 B.C., Aristotle was the son of the royal physician. At age 17, he left home to study at **Plato's Academy** in Athens. He remained there for 20 years, first as a student and later as a teacher.

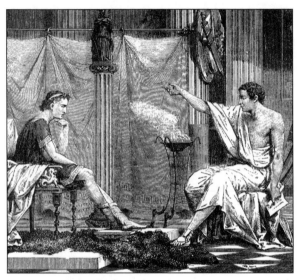

Aristotle and his pupil, Alexander

Around 345 B.C., Aristotle became the royal tutor of the 13-year-old Macedonian Prince, Alexander, who later became known as the world conqueror **Alexander the Great**. After Alexander was crowned king in 336 B.C., Aristotle returned to Athens and founded his own school, the **Lyceum**. He spent the next 13 years teaching and writing his philosophical, scientific, and political treatises.

The *Nicomachean Ethics* gets its name from Aristotle's son, **Nicomachus**, who recorded this version of his father's thoughts and notes on the subject of ethics. According to Aristotle, ethics refers to man's effort to find his highest good. All humans strive to achieve happiness, Aristotle believed, and for him hap-

piness is the activity of the soul in accordance with virtue.

Aristotle held the view that what separates humans from other species is reason. Employing reason to achieve happiness leads to moral virtues, such as courage, and to intellectual virtues, such as wisdom. Aristotle said that moral virtue is shown in the deliberate choice of actions as part of a worked-out plan of life; this plan should take a middle course between excess and deficiency. This is called the **doctrine of the golden mean**; for example, justice is the mean between a man getting more or less than what he deserves. Intellectual virtues, by contrast, were not subject to this doctrine of the golden mean.

Aristotle believed that a life of philosophical contemplation could bring a person supreme happiness. Yet Aristotle felt this state is only possible for a few. He believed that a kind of secondary happiness is available in a virtuous life of political activity and public good works.

Many of Aristotle's writings were hidden after his death to protect them from theft, but volumes were damaged by dampness and insects. The surviving books were discovered more than two centuries later and brought to Athens. When Romans captured Athens, the books were taken to Rome, where they attracted great attention among scholars.

During the Dark Ages, when the Catholic church banned or locked up classical works, Aristotle's writings were forgotten. In 1169, a Muslim scholar, **Ibn-Rushd**, translated Aristotle's works from Greek to Arabic to Latin, leading to a renewal of interest in Aristotle when the works were reintroduced in Europe.

10. On the Republic
(51 B.C.) Marcus Tullius Cicero

When America's founding fathers sought independence from Great Britain in 1776, they drew inspiration from *On the Republic*, the brilliant work by **Marcus Tullius Cicero**, the noted Roman statesman and orator who lived during the last days of the **Roman Republic**.

In the Declaration of Independence, **Thomas Jefferson** wrote, "We hold these truths to be self-evident, that all men are created equal."

In *De Re Publica* (*On The Republic*), Scipio, a character introduced by Cicero, drew the same conclusion: "Certainly equality of rights must subsist for all who are citizens of the same state. . ."

Cicero wrote *On The Republic* on papyrus scrolls in 51 B.C. In this work, Cicero describes the ideal commonwealth, and at the same time demonstrates that the Roman Republic had reached an increasing state of perfection as a government. It combined elements of monarchy, aristocracy, and democracy in the right balance. However, Cicero warned that this government could be destroyed—and was in danger of being so—by the moral decay of the aristocracy.

Such decay, Cicero believed, could lead to tyranny. Decrying tyranny, he said, "The essential justice that binds human society together and is maintained by one law is right reason . . . Whoever disregards this law, whether written or unwritten, is unjust."

Cicero went on to state that, "Where there is a tyranny . . . reason now compels us to maintain that there is no state at all." When a government fails to protect people or property, Cicero argued, citizens have the right to overthrow tyrants.

Similarly, in The Declaration of Independence, Jefferson states that when citizens' rights are abused by a despot, "it is their duty to throw off such government."

Cicero was born in 106 B.C., and raised and educated in Rome. He learned about the famous Greek orators, and also studied philosophy, literature, and law. In his twenties, he became a lawyer, defending citizens against injustices. Later, he joined the Senate and became a famous orator.

The murder of Cicero

Cicero spoke out against dishonest rulers. Following Julius Caesar's assassination in the Roman Senate in 45 B.C., Cicero delivered his famous **Philippics**—a condemnation of Marc Antony, one of the men vying to succeed Caesar, for inciting a civil war.

Cicero fled to Greece, where he was captured and killed. His head and hands were chopped off and nailed to the Senate rostrum in Rome, grim warnings to others not to dare criticize those who hold power.

Cicero's sentiments in *On the Republic* lived on, inspiring the **American War for Independence** and later, the **French Revolution**. Two thousand years after his death, Cicero's legacy endures, embodied in democratic republics around the world.

11. Koran
(c. A.D. 652)

Reading from the *Koran*

The *Koran* (or *Qur'an*), is the Holy Scripture of **Muslims**, who believe it is the word of **Allah**, God of the Islamic faith, as revealed to the prophet, **Muhammad**.

Muhammad was born in Mecca, an Arabian trading center, in A.D. 570 He was a humble man known for helping poor people. According to Muslim belief, the angel Gabriel appeared in a cave near Mecca and whispered Allah's words to Muhammad. Muhammad repeated aloud the revelation that there was one true God and called for destruction of idols worshiped by the Meccans.

Muhammad began to attract many followers, and according to Islamic tradition, received more revelations, spanning 20 years. He became a religious and political leader, and eventually established a state governed by **Islamic law**. He lived to see the spread of Islam throughout Arabia before his death in A.D. 632.

The *Koran*, which means "recitation," is believed by Muslims to be the precise word of God recited by Muhammad. The *Koran* teaches that through surrender (islam) to God, man can achieve salvation on Judgment Day. The *Koran* accepts Abraham, Moses, and Jesus Christ as prophets, but teaches that the word of God as revealed to Muhammad takes precedence over older prophecies, and that Islam is the one true religion. The *Koran* also defines **divine law (Sharia)**, which prescribes most aspects of private and social life for Muslims. Devout Muslims recite prayers five times daily, and aspire to make a holy pilgrimage to Mecca in their lifetime. The faith prescribes rituals, such as fasting during the month of Ramadan, and aspects of daily life, such as the role of women in Islamic society.

The first written copy of the *Koran* was probably made by a commission appointed by the third caliph—supreme leader—20 years after Muhammad's death. Although translations have been made, recitations must be performed in Arabic, the language of the *Koran*, since it is believed to represent the word of God. Purification rituals must be performed before handling the sacred text.

The growth of Islam significantly impacted world history. After Muhammad established the first Islamic society in Medina, the new religion spread swiftly. Decades after Muhammad's death, Islamic armies toppled the Byzantine Empire, conquering Egypt, Syria, Mesopotamia, and Iran to establish an Islamic Empire. Further conquests pushed Islam's borders west to Spain and east to India. Peaceful contacts, including those by Muslim traders, spread Islam throughout much of Africa.

At the turn of the 21st century, the Muslim world extended from Central Asia south to Africa and from Morocco east to the Philippines. The 1.15 billion followers of the Islamic faith comprise one-fifth of the earth's population.

12. The Tale of Genji
(c.1010) Murasaki Shikibu

The Tale of Genji, an 11th century Japanese story of romantic adventure, is considered by many historians to be the world's first novel.

Murasaki Shikibu, a lady-in-waiting to the Japanese Empress **Akiko**, wrote the story, which describes the romantic adventures of Prince Genji ("Shining Prince"). Shikibu's accurate descriptions of **Japanese court life** and of the aristocratic women wooed by the prince, reflect her own astute observations of the imperial family.

The tale explores themes of love, friendship, and filial loyalty. In the novel, a woman of lower rank in gives birth to a son named Genji. The emperor bestows favor upon Genji by taking the boy into the imperial court to be raised.

When Genji matures, he pursues many women, most of whom resist his advances, knowing no future can come of such a relationship. Genji even carries out secret affairs with women outside the court—actions considered scandalous. His romantic trysts prove at times humorous, at other times poignant.

Murasaki Shikibu

In one scene, Prince Genji makes negative comments about women who write fictitious tales. A female novelist character responds by offering a theory on how the art of novel writing began. "It happens because one's own experience of people and things has moved one to an emotion so passionate that it can no longer be shut up in one's heart. Again and again something in one's own life or in the lives of those around one will seem so important that the thought of letting it pass into oblivion is unbearable," the character replied, perhaps revealing Shikibu's motivations as well.

Shikibu's writing, which became more somber near the novel's conclusion, had Buddhist overtones, reflecting on the fleeting joys of earthly life. Some believe Shikibu may have sensed the eventual overthrow of the emperor by samurai warriors in the 12th century, an event that replaced imperialism with a feudal military government headed by a shogun.

Born in A.D. 973, Shikibu was the daughter of a provincial governor and well-known scholar.

Although it was considered improper for girls to learn to read during this time, Shikibu's father allowed her to study with her brother.

Shikibu married in her early twenties and gave birth to a daughter. Two years later, her husband died. The imperial family, impressed with Shikibu's intelligence and writing talent, invited the young widow to join the court as lady-in-waiting to the Empress Akiko.

Shikibu kept a diary for two years, recording vivid recollections of court life. Later, she completed *The Tale of Genji*, which became immediately popular. The novel has been translated into many languages and appreciated by people in many lands for its charm, literary quality, and accurate depictions of life in the Japanese imperial court.

13. The Travels of Marco Polo
(c.1300)   Marco Polo

The Travels of Marco Polo, Marco Polo's first-hand account of his travels in the **Orient** and adventures in **Kublai Khan's** court, led to the opening of Asian trade routes to Europeans, who eagerly sought spices, silks, and other treasures of the Far East.

The narrative later inspired **Christopher Columbus**, who used passages in *The Travels of Marco Polo* to chart his westward course. Columbus never found a sea route to the Orient, but without Polo's book as inspiration, he might never have sailed west to Asia— and discovered America instead.

Born in 1254 into a merchant family in **Venice**, Marco Polo didn't meet his father until he was 16 years old. His father and uncle were jewel merchants who had left Venice on a trading journey before Polo's birth. When war prevented their return, they journeyed east to the court of Kublai Khan, the powerful **Mongol** ruler of China.

On their next trip to Asia, they brought 17-year-old Marco with them; they spent the next 17 years in China. Marco Polo's skill as a storyteller pleased the Khan, who sent the young man on diplomatic missions throughout the empire.

When the Polos returned to Venice in 1295, Marco entranced the city's young people with his tales of exotic places. He became known as *il milione*, which meant "the man with a million stories."

Marco Polo

Polo became commander of a Venetian fleet, but was taken prisoner in 1298 during a sea battle against the Genoese navy. Jailed, he passed time by telling stories to other prisoners.

Polo dictated stories of his travels to a prisoner named **Rustichello**, who may have embellished the tales. Although some scholars have questioned the authenticity of certain descriptions, most historians now believe that Polo's detailed accounts of Mongol and Chinese society are accurate.

The book was published under several titles, including *Il Millione*, *The Book of Marvels*, and *The Travels of Marco Polo*. It became an instant success in medieval Europe. Scribes made copies by hand, translating it into many languages.

Freed from prison, Marco Polo returned to Venice, where he died in 1324. His colorful tales lived on, capturing the imagination of cartographers, merchants, and adventurers.

Following the invention of the printing press, the book became one of the first widely available to readers throughout Europe. With its accurate maps and wealth of information, it provided Europeans of the Middle Ages with their first substantial knowledge of China and parts of Asia. Seven hundred years after Polo dictated his travel memoirs in a Genoese prison, *The Tales of Marco Polo* remains a classic of travel literature.

14. The Divine Comedy
(c.1320) Dante Alighieri

The Divine Comedy, **Dante Alighieri's** epic narrative poem, is considered among the world's finest works of literature.

In this dramatic allegorical work, Dante vividly describes his imaginary journey through hell, purgatory, and heaven. During his spiritual quest, the poet encounters historical, mythological, and contemporary figures. Each character symbolizes a particular fault or virtue, resulting in punishments or rewards.

The Roman poet, Vergil, who represents reason, serves as Dante's guide through the Inferno (Hell), to free him of the temptation to sin, and Purgatory, to purify Dante's soul of even the capacity for error. Dante's portrayal of the nine circles of hell, culminating in an encounter with Lucifer, terrified medieval readers.

Beatrice, Dante's beloved, symbolizes divine revelation through faith. She guides Dante through Paradise, where he achieves purification of his soul and witnesses the glory of God. One of the most celebrated female characters in literature, Beatrice was inspired by a noblewoman whom Dante once loved.

Immensely popular, *The Divine Comedy* sparked a rediscovery of classical wisdom, igniting the **Italian Renaissance**. In addition to its religious significance, the work provides insights into the political and cultural climate of 13th century Italy.

Known to the literary world more familiarly by his given name, Dante was born in **Florence** in 1265. In his time, Florence was torn by conflict between imperial and papal supporters. Dante supported the latter group, and married the daughter of a prominent family from that faction. He was elected a prior, or magistrate, of Florence. During his term, he became involved in a political feud and was banished from Florence and ordered to pay a fine. When he failed to pay, he was condemned to death.

Dante lived in exile in Northern Italy and Paris, where he wrote works in Latin. For *The Divine Comedy,* however, he chose Italian, so that it could be widely read. He began the masterpiece around 1310, and completed it shortly before his death in exile in 1321.

The Divine Comedy became the first modern work taught along with ancient classics in universities. When the printing press was invented, 400 editions were published in Italian, which became the literary language in Western Europe for centuries. Printed editions attracted famed illustrators, including **Michelangelo** and **Botticelli**.

The Divine Comedy has been set to music by composers Peter Ilyich Tchaikovsky and Franz Liszt. It has been translated into more than 25 languages and inspired countless poets, including T.S. Eliot, who equated Dante's influence with that of playwright William Shakespeare.

Dante

21

15. Gutenberg Bible
(1455)

Johann Gutenberg, a German goldsmith, began an information revolution when he introduced **moveable type** to Europe and used his new press to print copies of the **Bible**.

The craft of printing dates back to the 8th century, when the Chinese began using carved wood blocks. Moveable type was also invented by the Chinese, but the process did not catch on in Asia, where writing required 10,000 separate characters.

When Gutenberg introduced moveable type to Europe, he adapted a screw press, which had been used for centuries to press oil from olives. He also invented printing ink, a thick paste-like substance made from lampblack and varnish.

The Bibles were published in **Latin** in three volumes. Each edition contained 42 lines per page set in two columns, using Gothic type with scrolled borders and two-color illuminated initials. Gutenberg printed 150 Bibles on paper and 30 more on parchment. Twenty still existed at the turn of the 21st century, including one in the Library of Congress.

The *Gutenberg Bible* contained the **Old Testament** and **New Testament**. The Old Testament (Latin for "covenant") included the Hebrew Scriptures of the Jewish Bible based on the "Old Covenant" believed to have been made by God with the people of Israel in ancient times. It included the story of creation (Genesis), rules and instructions (the Torah, or Pentateuch), collections of wisdoms (Proverbs), poetry (Psalms), and books of the prophets.

The New Testament included retellings of the acts and sayings of Jesus Christ (Gospels), historical narrative (Acts), letters of the apostles, and Revelations, which foretold the apocalypse, or end of the world.

The new technology revolutionized the dissemination of information. Prior to printing of the *Gutenberg Bible*, books were hand-copied by scribes, a laborious and costly process that limited book collecting to only wealthy individuals.

Gutenberg's invention enabled the written word to be reproduced quickly, cheaply, and in large quantities. Within 50 years after Gutenberg printed his first Bibles, more than ten million printed books had been published, including Greek and Roman classics, scientific works, and Columbus's report of the New World. Libraries became established and reading became a popular pastime among the middle class throughout Europe.

Gutenberg failed to profit from his monumental achievement, however. His heavy investment in the invention bankrupted him; in 1455, a creditor took over his business. Gutenberg died in 1468.

The impact of Gutenberg's invention, however, endured far beyond his lifetime. The printing press made the Bible widely available, spreading spiritual and moral concepts of Christianity throughout Europe. Gutenberg's printing press also helped fuel the **Renaissance**, the **Protestant Reformation**, the **Industrial Revolution**, and other significant events in the centuries to come.

Gutenberg using his press

16. The Prince

(1513) Niccolò Machiavelli

One of the world's most famous political treatises, *The Prince* has been used as a guide for rulers in gaining power by whatever means are necessary—and retaining it at all costs.

The Prince was written by **Niccolò Machiavelli**, a **Florentine** statesman and diplomat. In a radical departure from previous works on government, *The Prince* focused not on lofty ethical ideals, but instead provided practical—and devious—advice for a monarch seeking to stay in power.

Monarchs need not be bound by traditional ethical standards, Machiavelli argued. Instead, he counseled:

"Hence, it is necessary for a prince wishing to hold his own to know how to do wrong, and to make use of it or not according to necessity."

Machiavelli pointed out that certain "virtues" might lead to the downfall of a monarchy, whereas some "vices" might help a monarch to prosper. For example, a generous prince might risk going broke to maintain his reputation. Thus, it is better to cultivate a reputation for stinginess, Machiavelli maintained. Similarly, he argued that it is better for a monarch to be severe than merciful in doling out punishments, in order to deter crime. He also advised that a prince should learn how to be deceitful when necessary.

Machiavelli had ample opportunity to observe tactics employed by rulers. He was born in Florence in 1469, when Italy was divided between four city states. Machiavelli entered public service and became a diplomat for the Florentine Republic.

He also met and studied the political tactics of Italian rulers, including **Cesare Borgia**, who was rapidly expanding his holdings in central Italy. Within months, Borgia had conquered a dominion for himself, inspiring Machiavelli to adapt Borgia's methods to his own ideal of a "new prince" who might solve Italy's problems.

In 1512, when the powerful **Médici** family regained control of Florence and dissolved the Republic, Machiavelli was accused of conspiring against them. He was removed from office, imprisoned, and tortured. After his release from prison, he retired to his home near Florence, where he wrote *The Prince*. He died in 1527.

Some have questioned whether Machiavelli truly intended to aid dictators by advocating amoral actions, or whether *The Prince* may in fact have been meant as a satire, exposing ruthless tactics of monarchs to public scrutiny in order to protect the Republic.

Whichever the case, Machiavelli's work initiated a fundamental change in attitudes toward government. *The Prince*, now regarded as a basic text of political science, brought an end to humanism and the beginning of realism in the study of politics. The term **"Machiavellian"** has become a synonym for duplicity and political cunning.

Machiavelli

17. Utopia
(1516) Thomas More

Englishman Sir **Thomas More** was disturbed by conditions in 16th century Europe—at the time, a continent divided by greedy rulers interested in power and wealth. In 1516, he wrote *Utopia*, a satirical novel of a better life in an idyllic society.

In *Utopia*, a stranded traveler discovers the island of Utopia, a perfect state founded entirely on reason. There, individual interests are secondary to society's interests, religious tolerance is practiced, and education is provided for everyone. Land is owned by the people and everyone shares in the work.

Thomas More

More's idealized world was intended as sharp contrast to English society. For example, More described how the Utopians had once quarreled over religion. As a result, the ruler Utopus "made a law that every man might be of what religion he pleased," More wrote. Forcing beliefs on others would lead to banishment or slavery. The law was passed not only to assure peace, but also because Utopus suspected that different religions might "all come from God, who might inspire men in a different manner, and be pleased with this variety."

While the book begins with praise for England's King **Henry VIII**, More also writes ". . . there are many things in the Commonwealth of Utopia that I rather wish, than hope, to see followed in our governments." More used Socratic dialogues involving real people, including himself and his former teacher, **Cardinal Morton**. Some readers recognized the work as satire; others believed the state described was real—some people even proposed sending missionaries to the nonexistent island.

Thomas More was born in 1478; as a young man, he studied classics, theology and music. During the reign of King Henry VII, More became a member of Parliament. He later became a confidante of Henry's successor, his son, Henry VIII.

Around 1530, Henry VIII decided he wanted to divorce his wife, Catherine of Aragon, in order to remarry; however, the **Roman Catholic Church** refused permission. Determined to have his way, the king challenged the pope's authority and established a separate **Church of England** with himself as its leader.

More could not condone the king's actions. He resigned his office and refused to take a loyalty oath required of all English subjects. More would not relent, even after Henry imprisoned him for 15 months.

His convictions cost More his life. Charged with treason, he was beheaded in 1535. Viewed as a martyr by the Catholic Church, More was **canonized** four centuries after his death.

The phrase "**Utopian**" has come to be synonymous with an idealized, if unattainable, social system. Translated into many languages, *Utopia* has inspired countless other books envisioning a perfect social order.

18. Ninety-five Theses

(1517) Martin Luther

When **Martin Luther** nailed his *Ninety-five Theses* to the door of a church in Wittenberg, Germany in 1517, his harsh criticism of practices of the Catholic Church led to the **Protestant Reformation**—a movement that created a "religious earthquake" within Christianity.

The son of a copper miner, Luther was born in 1483. Over his father's objections, he entered a monastery and was ordained as a Catholic priest at age 20. He went on to study at **Wittenberg University**, where he became chairman of biblical theology.

In *Ninety-five Theses*, Luther criticized the Vatican for selling **indulgences**—promises to forgive sins—in exchange for donations. Indulgences were granted by the pope and made available through church representatives. Pope **Sixtus IV** extended the scope of indulgences, making it possible to also buy forgiveness for souls in purgatory. By the Middle Ages, abuses of some indulgence sellers had become widespread.

Believing that redemption and the power of mercy belonged to God, not the Church, Luther denounced the sale of indulgences. Luther wrote that those who believe they can be certain of their salvation because they have indulgence letters will be forever damned, together with their teachers. The pope had no authority over purgatory, he argued, adding that unbridled preaching of indulgences makes it difficult even for learned men to rescue the reverence which is due the pope from slander or from the shrewd questions of the laity. . . such as, "Why does not the pope empty purgatory for the sake of holy love and the dire need of the souls that are there. . ."

In *Ninety-five Theses*, Luther also argued that Scripture, or Biblical texts, should take precedence over Church doctrine. He denied the infallibility of popes and Church coun-

Martin Luther

cils—and quickly found his ideas denounced as **heresy**.

Knowledge of Luther's beliefs spread rapidly, as copies of *Ninety-five Theses* were produced on printing presses and distributed, provoking strong controversy.

The Vatican summoned Luther to Rome, but he refused to go. In 1521, the pope **excommunicated** Luther on charges of heresy. He was banned from the empire, and his books were burned. Undeterred, he continued his rebellion against Church doctrine.

Hiding in a German castle, he translated the New Testament from Greek into German. Distribution of his translation increased his followers, and he continued writing on theological matters.

Luther died in 1546, and after his death, his followers took up his cause. They spread a new form of Christianity throughout Europe, ultimately giving birth to the Protestant denomination. The Reformation sparked by Luther's *Ninety-five Theses* fomented great religious, social, and political changes for centuries to come.

25

The Fabric of the Human Body
(1543) Andreas Vesalius

Andreas Vesalius, a **Belgian** physician, published the first accurate book on human **anatomy**. Based on his observations from dissections of human cadavers, *De Humani Corporis Fabrica Libri Septem (The Fabric of the Human Body)* corrected misperceptions held since ancient times and revolutionized the field of anatomy.

Born in 1514 into a family of physicians in Brussels, Vesalius was the son of the well-respected apothecary to Emperor Maximilian I of the Hapsburg family.

At the University of Paris, Vesalius became fascinated by anatomy. He dissected animals, gaining respect of his teachers for his attention to detail. He also dissected human cadavers obtained from Paris cemeteries. Later he went to Padua, Italy, where he earned a medical degree and was appointed professor of surgery and anatomy.

A student of the classics, Vesalius believed modern anatomy was a revival of classical anatomy. Thus, he was shocked when his observations led him to conclude that **Galen**, the respected 2nd century anatomist and physician to the gladiators, had never dissected a human corpse. Instead, Vesalius believed, Galen had based his deductions regarding human anatomy entirely on dissections of animals. Galen, though accurate on some matters, had made some faulty premises.

In 1543, Vesalius published his seven-volume work, including 300 illustrations of human skeletal, muscular, and nervous systems. Vesalius detailed his own discoveries, and corrected more than 200 errors he had found in Galen's books. For example, through dissections, Vesalius learned that the jaw is one bone, not two. He also found that men and women have an equal numbers of ribs.

Vesalius also omitted depiction of Asclepius' rod and serpent. Although Vesalius viewed modern anatomy as a resurrection of classical anatomy, he chose science over mysticism, rejecting magical cures attributed to Asclepius' medical symbol.

Anatomy, Vesalius maintained, "should be recalled from the dead, so that. . . one could with confidence assert that our modern science of anatomy was equal to that of old, and that in this age anatomy was unique both in the level to which it had sunk and in the completeness of its subsequent restoration."

Publication of his books provoked a firestorm of controversy. Followers of Galen turned against Vesalius, ridiculing him as a madman. Depressed by the slanderous statements made about him, Vesalius burned portions of his works.

After Vesalius's death in a shipwreck in 1564, a pupil, **Realdo Columbus**, continued his work, making important discoveries about blood circulation and respiration. In later years, respect grew for Vesalius, who has come to be known as the **father of modern anatomy**.

Andreas Vesalius

20. On the Revolutions of the Celestial Spheres (1543) Nicolaus Copernicus

In his historic scientific work, *On the Revolutions of the Celestial Spheres*, Polish astronomer **Nicolaus Copernicus** proposed a radical concept of the Earth's relationship to the sun that dramatically altered man's perception of his world and the universe.

Before Copernicus, people believed that Earth was the center of the universe. Ptolemy, the ancient Egyptian astronomer, and Aristotle, the Greek philosopher, had expounded this geocentric view. However, as astronomers and scientists of the Middle Ages made new discoveries about planetary behavior, using this theory presented problems and left unexplained certain astronomical observations.

Copernicus proposed an even more startling idea: that the sun is the center of the universe, with Earth and other planets revolving around the sun.

Born into a merchant family in 1473, Copernicus began his studies in Poland. Later, he studied medicine, law, astronomy, and mathematical sciences in Italy. He returned to Poland in 1506 to serve as a private physician to his uncle, a Catholic bishop.

In his spare time, Copernicus applied mathematics to astronomy to calculate planetary positions and predict the times of celestial events such as eclipses. Around 1513, Copernicus wrote a brief version of his **heliocentric (sun-centered)** theory, known as the *Commentarius*.

Over the years, Copernicus perfected his theory. His confidence in his view of the planetary system was bolstered by new evidence. For example, astronomers observed that over a period of two years Mars faded from a bright red to a dimmer one. An Earth-centered system offered no explanation for this fact. However, in a sun-centered system, if Earth and Mars traveled around the sun at different speeds, they would sometimes be close together, and that would cause Mars to appear brighter at times.

Copernicus hesitated for more than 10 years before he published his theory. His reluctance was due to fear of reprisal by the **Catholic Church**, which viewed any scientific challenge to Scripture or to the writings of the Church fathers as heretical.

Copernicus

Finally, in 1543, Copernicus published his findings. The sun-centered universe proposal was so controversial that the printer, a German Lutheran, felt obliged to protect himself by adding a forward from a Lutheran priest stating the work was only a theory.

The first copy of the book, *De Revolutionibus Orbium Coelestium (On the Revolutions of the Celestial Spheres)*, arrived on May 24, 1543, as Copernicus lay desperately ill. He died of a stroke shortly after receiving the book.

For 50 years, Copernican theory failed to gain popularity—until Italian astronomer **Galileo Galilei** built a large telescope in 1609. Within a year, his observations confirmed that the Copernican system was correct.

21. Romeo and Juliet
(1594) William Shakespeare

Of all the works of the world's most famous dramatist—English playwright and poet **William Shakespeare**—perhaps none has achieved more universal appeal than his tragic tale of young star-crossed lovers, *Romeo and Juliet.*

Set in Verona, Italy, in the late 15th century, the play depicts the ill-fated love affair between Romeo, son of the **House of Montague**, and Juliet, daughter of the **Capulet** family.

Romeo and Juliet meet at a masked ball. They fall in love, although their families are feuding. In the garden beneath Juliet's balcony, Romeo overhears her vow to forsake her family for love:

"O Romeo, Romeo!" said she, "wherefore art thou Romeo? Deny thy father, and refuse thy name, for my sake; or if thou wilt not, be but my sworn love, and I no longer will be a Capulet."

Since Juliet's parents have arranged for her to wed a count, Romeo and Juliet marry in secret. Soon after, Romeo is forced to avenge his friend's death by slaying Juliet's cousin. Banished for his deed, Romeo finds refuge with Friar Laurence.

Juliet seeks help from the friar, who gives her a sleeping potion to make her appear dead. After she is brought to the Capulet vault for burial, she is to awaken and be found by Romeo.

When Romeo slips into the tomb, however, he is devastated to find Juliet apparently dead and he commits suicide. Juliet awakens, heartbroken at Romeo's death, and kills herself with his dagger. Horrified by their children's deaths, the Capulets and the Montagues end their feud.

Writing with a great sense of drama, Shakespeare explored the role of fortune, as well as the consequences of hostility and deception. In classic fashion, he created a tragic hero whose rashness and passion result in his destruction and that of the one he loves most.

The story's timeless appeal has assured its endurance long past Shakespeare's day. Since its first performance around 1594, *Romeo and Juliet* has been presented countless times on stages worldwide, and made into movies several times. During the 1950s, it was modernized—on stage and film—into a 20th century musical, *West Side Story*, depicting young lovers from different backgrounds whose families belong to rival gangs in New York City.

Born in England in 1564, Shakespeare left his home at Stratford-on-Avon in 1588 and moved to London. He became an actor, formed an acting company, and acquired part ownership of the **Globe Theater**. He soon established a reputation as a poet and as a playwright. Shakespeare's plays were often performed at the court of Queen **Elizabeth I**. He retired in 1611 to Stratford, where he died in 1616.

William Shakespeare

Don Quixote de la Mancha
(1605) Miguel de Cervantes

Miguel de Cervantes's, *Don Quixote de la Mancha* is considered the first modern novel, and has served as a model for much of the world's fiction.

In de Cervantes' day, popular fiction consisted largely of romantic tales from the Middle Ages. In those stories, wandering knights in shining armor upheld the code of chivalry, performing good deeds while protecting damsels in distress.

Recognizing that chivalry had become outdated, Cervantes wrote a parody of chivalric practices. In *Don Quixote*, a deluded nobleman sets out to become a knight errant, intent on combating injustices. Though clearly a satire, the novel is also viewed as an allegory of man's eternal quest for truth and virtue despite impossible obstacles. Heroism equates with insanity, leading some to term the novel a tragedy.

Quixote's imagination borders on madness as he pursues his quest astride his horse, **Rocinante.** His idealism is tempered by the realistic outlook of his squire, **Sancho Panza**, an uneducated peasant.

"Look there, friend Sancho Panza, where thirty or more monstrous giants rise up, all of whom I mean to engage in battle and slay," Quixote observes.

The squire hastily points out that Quixote has mistaken windmills for giants, but is unable to prevent his master's next action:

"With lance braced and covered by his shield, he charged at Rocinante's fullest gallop and attacked the first mill that stood in front of him. But as he drove his lance-point into the sail, the wind whirled it around with such force that it shivered the lance to pieces. It swept away with it horse and rider, and they were sent rolling over the plain, in sad condition indeed."

Cervantes was born in 1547, son of a poor doctor. As a young man, he served as a soldier, until his arm was injured during a battle. When he was in his thirties, he began to write poems and plays, but was unable to support himself. He went to work for the government, furnishing goods to the Spanish fleet. Later, Cervantes became a tax collector, but was imprisoned for collection irregularities. He may have begun writing *Don Quixote* in his jail cell.

In 1605, he published the book, which became an immediate success. After an unauthorized sequel appeared, Cervantes decided to publish his own sequel in 1615, two years before his death. The two volumes were later combined into one book.

The novel has been translated into more than 60 languages. *Don Quixote* has inspired paintings, an opera, a motion picture, and a Broadway musical, *Man of La Mancha*. Cervantes's literary characters remain among the most enduring of all time.

Miguel de Cervantes

23. Treatise on Painting
(1651) Leonardo da Vinci

Leonardo da Vinci was one of the world's greatest artists, creator of the masterpieces *Mona Lisa* and *The Last Supper*. More than a century after his death, his extensive notebooks, detailing his **artistic techniques** and his advice to aspiring painters, were published in his *Treatise on Painting*.

Born in 1452, da Vinci apprenticed as a youth with a famed Florentine sculptor and painter. Experimenting with mixing colors, da Vinci taught himself to paint with oils. Soon, he surpassed his master, creating startling life-like figures.

While working in Milan, da Vinci began writing texts for his apprentices and pupils. However, his notebooks, more than 1,000 pages of observations and illustrations, remained unpublished for more than a century after his death in 1519.

In 1651, his *Treatise on Painting* was compiled. It details techniques on perspective, light and shadow, color, glazing, and paint-mixing.

"The painter must keep ten things in mind to ensure the success of his work—namely, light, shadow, color, volume, form, placing, distance, proximity, movement, and repose," wrote da Vinci.

"Painting consists of the outline which surrounds the forms and painted objects, which we call drawing, and shadow," he wrote. He urged painters to imitate nature and criticized artists who endowed children with adult proportions. To assure accurate depictions, he advised examining a model's reflection in a mirror. To achieve perspective, he suggested deepening blues in distant objects and using "pyramidal trajectories."

On lighting, da Vinci said, "Shadow is of the nature of darkness; light is of the nature of splendor. They are always combined on the body, and shadow is more powerful than light, for it can completely exclude light and deprive bodies of it entirely, while light can never eliminate all shadows from bodies, at least from opaque bodies."

Colors vary depending on conditions, he noted. "Blacks have the most beauty in shadow, whites in the light, and the blues, greens and browns in medium shadow, the yellows and reds in the light, the gold in reflections, and the lakes in medium shadow."

Da Vinci also offered specific instructions:

To contrast clothing on mortals and heavenly beings, he advised, " . . . you will reveal the exact dimensions of the limbs only in the case of nymphs or angels, which are represented draped in fine cloth, adhering to and molding their limbs in the wind."

Ironically, although da Vinci alluded to his famed **chiaroscuro method**, his manuscript was illusive on details. Modern science, however, has solved the mystery through color-matching da Vinci's **Renaissance** palette and glazing techniques, revealing secrets of the Old Master, whose beautiful, realistic style continues to influence artists nearly 500 years after his death.

Raphael meets da Vinci

24. The Pilgrim's Progress
(1678;1684)   John Bunyan

The Pilgrim's Progress is a religious allegory, a symbolic tale depicting a good man's pilgrimage in search of salvation. At one time, this story, written by **John Bunyan**, was second only to the Bible in popularity, read throughout Europe as well as in the American colonies.

The Pilgrim's Progress is written in Biblical-style prose in two parts; Part I describes a dream in which **Christian** travels from the **City of Destruction** to the **Celestial City**. Along the way, he encounters characters aptly described by names such as Faithful, Hopeful, Sloth, Obstinate, and Mr. Worldly Wiseman. Upon encountering Sloth in fetters, for example, Christian tries to help free the man from the leg irons that confine him. But Sloth replies, "Yet a little more sleep."

Part II recounts attempts by Christian's wife and sons to join him in the Celestial City, along with some new companions, such as Mr. Ready-to-halt and Mrs. Much-afraid.

On one level, *The Pilgrim's Progress* provided an entertaining story. On another, it offered a religious message to entice readers to save their souls. In the author's "apology" for his book, Bunyan writes:

"This book will make a traveller of thee,
If by its counsel thou wilt rule be;
It will direct thee to the Holy Land,
If thou wilt its directions understand:
Yea, it will make the slothful active be;
The blind also delightful things to see."

Born in England in 1628, John Bunyan was the son of a tinker who was devoutly religious. As a young man, Bunyan fought in the Parliamentary army of Oliver Cromwell and became involved with the **Puritan** religious movement.

In 1653, Bunyan became a Baptist and the leader of a congregation, giving sermons as a lay preacher. When the monarchy was restored and King Charles II claimed the throne in 1660, religious persecution ensued; conduct-

John Bunyan

ing any religious service that did not conform to the **Church of England's** doctrines was declared illegal.

Bunyan refused to stop preaching sermons. As a result, he was arrested and thrown in jail for 12 years. While in prison, he began writing religious works.

Three years after his release from jail, Bunyan was imprisoned again. During this time, he began writing his greatest work, *The Pilgrim's Progress From This World to That Which Is to Come*. Part I was published in 1678; Part II in 1684. Freed from prison, Bunyan died in 1688.

The Pilgrim's Progress has been translated into many languages and strongly influenced later English writers. Its simple, homespun style, folktale-like qualities, and religious message combined to make Bunyan's allegorical tale one of the most widely read books in the English language.

One of the most important scientific works in history, **Isaac Newton's** *Philosophiae Naturalis Principia Mathematica (Mathematical Principles of Natural Philosophy)* defined **laws of motion** and provided explanations for mysteries that had baffled scientists for centuries.

Before Newton's time, no one knew why objects always fell to earth, what caused the tides, or how the planets were held in their orbits. Reportedly, after observing an apple fall from a tree, Newton concluded that **gravitational forces** accounted for each of these phenomena.

Before Newton, astronomers had been baffled over how to determine planetary orbits. In a meeting with English astronomer **Edmund Halley** (the discoverer of Halley's Comet), Newton suggested that the shape of an orbit based on the inverse square of the distance between the sun and its planets would produce an ellipse. Newton devised formulas to explain this and other laws of motion, which he published in 1689 in *Principia*.

Originally written and published in Latin, the book introduced the concept that the effects of gravity extend throughout the solar system. Gravity accounted for the flow of tides, motions of the Moon, and variations in the onset of seasons from year to year, Newton wrote. His law of gravitation used dynamics, or laws of nature governing motion and its effect on bodies, to create a mechanical basis for the workings of the universe.

A perfectionist who believed in thoroughly testing his theories, Newton waited many years after making his initial studies before publishing the *Principia*. It was hailed as a masterpiece by the scientific community.

Born on Christmas Day, 1642, at Woolsthorpe, Lincolnshire in England, Newton spent his early years at his grandmother's home, since his father died before he was born. At the age of ten, he was sent to school in a neighboring town, where he lived with an apothecary. There, Newton developed a lifelong interest in science.

After studying mathematics and science at Trinity College, Cambridge, Newton returned to Woolsthorpe in 1665, where he conducted research and made landmark discoveries in **optics** and motion. He returned to Cambridge and became a professor, lecturing while continuing his studies of gravitation.

Newton's genius extended beyond physics. He also founded the science of optics after using a prism to discover that white light is a mixture of every color in the spectrum. He invented the first **reflecting telescope**. In addition, Newton created **calculus**, an advanced form of calculations in mathematics.

Newton's laws of motion described in *Principia* form the foundation of modern physics. His discoveries later led to Einstein's theory of relativity, and to the development of quantum theory, further illuminating the physical laws governing the universe.

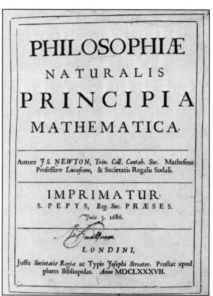

PHILOSOPHIÆ

NATURALIS

PRINCIPIA

MATHEMATICA.

Autore *JS. NEWTON,* Trin. Coll. Cantab. Soc. Matheseos Professore Lucasiano, & Societatis Regalis Sodali.

IMPRIMATUR·

S. PEPYS, Reg. Soc. PRÆSES.

Julii 5. 1686.

LONDINI,

Jussu Societatis Regiæ ac Typis *Josephi* Streater. Prostat apud plures Bibliopolas. *Anno* MDCLXXXVII.

Front cover of Newton's book

26. Two Treatises of Government
(1690) John Locke

During one of the most turbulent eras in English history, philosopher **John Locke** witnessed the effects of an oppressive monarchy—and of revolution. In 1690, he published *Two Treatises of Government*, promoting concepts of liberty and freedom that have become foundations of **democracy** around the world.

Locke attacked the divine right of kings, arguing that sovereignty resides not in the state, but with the people. Like the great Roman writer and orator **Cicero**, Locke insisted that citizens have a right to revolt against a tyrannical government:

" . . . those who were forced to submit to the yoke of government by constraint, have always a right to shake it off, and free themselves from the usurpation of tyranny. . ."

Nearly a century later, Locke's words from *Two Treatises* influenced America's founding fathers, who incorporated his ideas into the two documents that formed the foundation of the government of the United States—the **Declaration of Independence** and the **Constitution**.

Locke believed that government must obey civil and natural law. He defined the pursuit of life, liberty and property as inalienable natural rights—a phrase **Thomas Jefferson** closely paralleled when he wrote the Declaration of Independence.

Locke also advocated a system of checks and balances to prevent any single branch of government from becoming too powerful. He

believed in separation of church and state to protect religious freedom. Those principles were later embodied in the U.S. Constitution.

Locke's ideals were forged during violent times. In 1649, when Locke was 17, King Charles I was beheaded by English Puritans. The ensuing chaos culminated in the reign of Oliver Cromwell, the first commoner to rule England.

In 1660, the Catholic ruler, Charles (II) Stuart, claimed the throne, restoring the monarchy. Locke became physician and advisor to the powerful Earl of Shaftsbury, a leader of the Whigs, a political party that opposed the king.

The political climate in England forced Locke to flee with Shaftsbury in exile to Holland in 1683; Locke returned to England at the end of the decade after the "Glorious Revolution" restored the Protestants to power in 1688. He published his most famous works, *Essay Concerning Human Understanding* and *Two Treatises of Government*, in 1690. He died in 1704.

Locke's writings had a profound influence on the philosophers and writers of the **Age of Enlightenment**, a movement that developed later in the 18th century. Locke's words helped spark the **American Revolution** in 1775 and the **French Revolution** of 1789. His ideals have since been immortalized in documents of democracy, earning Locke a reputation as the **"philosopher of freedom."**

John Locke

27. Robinson Crusoe
(1719)   Daniel Defoe

Robinson Crusoe, **Daniel Defoe's** tale of a shipwrecked sailor's adventures, established a realistic style of fiction, setting the tone for the modern English novel.

Daniel Defoe

Before Defoe, stories were generally told as long poems or dramatic plays. In Spain, **Miguel de Cervantes** had broken with tradition by writing *Don Quixote* (see no. 22) in narrative form, but that satire used idealistic, not realistic, characters. By contrast, Defoe used first-person narrative in the form of journal entries to create a new genre of fiction: the **realistic novel.**

The novel describes Crusoe's struggle to survive after being shipwrecked on an island off **South America**. Crusoe is introduced as a young man yearning for adventure. However, after the shipwreck, he evolves spiritually, emotionally, and physically during the 28 years before his rescue.

At first, he is overwhelmed by isolation, but survives through his ingeniousness. For instance, this diary entry reveals how he salvaged materials from the ship:

"May 5— Worked on the wreck, cut another beam asunder, and brought three great fir-plans off from the decks, which I tied together, and made swim on shore, when the tide of flood came on."

Crusoe learns to accept and embrace solitude—until several years after the shipwreck, when he finds a man's footprint on the sand. The discovery upends his world, as this journal entry reveals:

"I stood like one thunder-struck, or as if I had seen an apparition. . . How came it to be thither I knew not, nor could in the least imagine. But after innumerable fluttering thoughts, like a man perfectly confused and out of myself, I came home to my fortification . . . terrified to the last degree. . ."

Crusoe draws on his faith for sustenance, resolving to "pray earnestly to God for deliverance." Yet when he is joined on the island by another man, **Friday**, Crusoe endures conflicting sentiments over the prospect of human companionship.

Defoe based the novel in part on stories told by **Alexander Selkirk**, a marooned British sailor whom Defoe may have once interviewed.

Defoe was born in 1660 in London. He studied to become a Presbyterian minister, but became a merchant instead. Late in life he turned to writing. Defoe's most famous novel, originally titled, *The Life and Strange Surprizing Adventures of Robinson Crusoe, of York, Mariner*, was published in 1719, when he was nearly 60 years old.

Defoe's story of the marooned mariner has fascinated generations of readers with its vivid descriptions and commentary on the human need for both society and solitude. *Robinson Crusoe* also inspired later writers of adventurous tales, including **Jules Verne** and **Robert Louis Stevenson**.

28. Poor Richard's Almanack

(1732-1757)   Benjamin Franklin

During the period leading up to the War for Independence, *Poor Richard's Almanack*, created by one of America's most noted figures, gained widespread popularity among readers, who enjoyed its wry humor and homespun wisdom.

Poor Richard, a simple country dweller who offered practical yet witty proverbs, was a character created by **Benjamin Franklin**, a self-educated printer who later became a statesman, diplomat, and one of the founding fathers of the United States.

Franklin published the first volume of *Poor Richard's Almanack* under the pen name **Richard Saunders**. Franklin introduced the almanack's fictitious author with a letter that would duplicate the book's wry and subtle humor.

"Courteous Reader,

I might in this place attempt to gain thy Favour, by declaring that I write Almanacks with no other View than that of the publick Good; but in this I should not be sincere. . . The plain Truth of the Matter is, I am excessive poor, and my Wife, good Woman is, I tell her, excessive proud; she cannot bear, she says, to sit spinning in her Shift of Tow, while I do nothing but gaze at the Stars; and has threatened more than once to burn all my Books and Rattling-Traps (as she calls my instruments) if I do not make some profitable Use of them for the good of my Family. The Printer has offer'd me some considerable share of the Profits . . . the Buyer of my Almanack may consider himself, not only as purchasing an useful Utensil, but as performing an Act of Charity, to his poor
Friend and Servant

R.Saunders."

In addition to a calendar and annual weather forecast for the year, the almanack contained amusing stories and proverbs promoting values of thrift and hard work.

One of his best-known proverbs advised, "Early to bed and early to rise, makes a man healthy, wealthy, and wise." Others displayed wry wit: "Fish and visitors smell in three days."

Franklin's origins were as humble as those of the character he created. Born in 1706 to a poor family in Boston, he was one of 17 children. At 13, he became an apprentice for his older brother, James, a printer.

Franklin moved to Philadelphia in 1723. Six years later, he bought the **Pennsylvania Gazette**, a newspaper he quickly transformed with his witty, informative style. In 1732, he published the first volume of the almanack.

Franklin's creation, Poor Richard, displayed rustic humor and ordinary common sense, characteristics that had great appeal to a large segment of readers in colonial America.

Ben Franklin

29. The Social Contract
(1762) Jean Jacques Rousseau

"Man was born free, but he is everywhere in chains," **Jean Rousseau** wrote in the famous opening line of *The Social Contract.*

The controversial volume incited the **French Revolution** of 1789 and became the Bible of the revolutionaries, who adopted the book's phrase, "**Liberty, Equality, Fraternity**" as their slogan.

Rousseau's works—and the revolution that ensued—hastened an end to the **Age of Enlightenment**. By arguing that emotion and subjective experience were as respectable as reason, Rousseau heralded a change in European thought and served as a catalyst for the era of **Romanticism** in the 19th century.

Born in 1712 in Geneva, Switzerland, Rousseau settled in Paris when he was 20. There he held a variety of jobs, from music teacher to political secretary, as well as a writer of operas.

In 1750, Rousseau won an award from the Academy of Dijon for his *Discourse on the Sciences and the Arts*, which claimed that art and science corrupted mankind. In 1755, he published a second controversial work, *Discourse on the Origin and Foundation of Inequality*, in which he argued that man's natural or primitive state is superior to the civilized state.

In 1762, Rousseau published his infamous political treatise, *The Social Contract.* The work was divided into four books. The first addressed the formation of societies and what Rousseau described as the "social contract" or compact to which people agree as a condition of living in a society. The second dealt with the rights of sovereigns, the third with the exercise of democracy, and the fourth with social institutions, such as the Church.

When a state fails to act in a moral fashion, Rousseau maintained, it ceases to exert authority over individuals. True law must be based on just law made by the people. He inflamed revolutionists passions with phrases such as "To renounce liberty is to renounce being a man, to surrender the rights of humanity and even its duties."

Jean Jacques Rousseau

Rousseau's fiery rhetoric in *The Social Contract* invoked the wrath of both French and Swiss authorities, forcing him to flee to Prussia and later, to England. He returned to France in 1768 under a false name and made a modest living as a copyist.

Rousseau did not live to witness the fuse that he'd ignited explode in the French Revolution of 1787. Mentally unstable, the revolutionary author sought shelter in a hospital and died in 1778, possibly by suicide.

Rousseau's writings not only had a radical influence upon the political landscape of Europe following his death, but also sparked the development of romanticism in literature and philosophy during the next century.

30. Inquiry into the Nature and Causes of the Wealth of Nations (1776) Adam Smith

While Great Britain and America were engaged in the Revolutionary War in 1776, **Adam Smith** was creating another kind of revolution, and his classic treatise, *Inquiry into the Nature and Causes of the Wealth of Nations*, established a foundation for **modern economics**.

Smith, a Scottish philosopher and political economist, presented the merits of free trade in an era when the British public and Parliament clung to **mercantilism**, a feudal economic system in which the government maintained protectionist controls over the national economy.

In *Wealth of Nations*, Smith called for economic freedom, also known as free trade or a **laissez-faire economy**, in both Britain and America, rejecting mercantilism of the past. The book also explored concepts of self-interest, division of labor, market functions, and international aspects of free trade. Smith argued that state efforts to control the economy had little impact compared with a free market economy.

In a competitive free market, Smith maintained, each individual could exert only a minimal influence on prices, yet the sum of all individuals' actions could profoundly impact pricing. This "invisible hand" of the market, Smith observed, served as an instrument to convert "private vices," such as greed, into "public virtues," such as maximum production. Smith's theories provided an objective means of studying economic behavior, giving rise to the science of economics.

Adam Smith

In Britain, Parliament and the public were slow to reject mercantilism for many years after Smith's death in 1790. However, his concepts were embraced in America following the Revolution.

Smith was born in 1723 at Kirkcaldy, Fife, Scotland. His father was comptroller of customs in Kirkcaldy, giving Smith an early introduction to economics.

At age 15, Smith attended Glasgow University, where he studied moral philosophy. Later, he attended Balliol College, Oxford. He became a lecturer in Edinburgh, speaking frequently on his favorite topic, the "progress of opulence." He discussed his economic theory of the "simple system of natural liberty," a philosophy later expanded in *Wealth of Nations*.

In 1759, he published *Theory of Moral Sentiments*, which discussed ethical standards of conduct needed to bind society together. Subsequently, he shifted his focus to political economics. After traveling abroad for several years, Smith returned home, and spent a decade preparing his monumental work. In 1776, he moved to London, where he published *Wealth of Nations*.

Smith's work incorporated his own ideas along with those of other intellectuals of his day, notably **David Hume** and **Montesquieu**. *Wealth of Nations* was the first book published on political economics and remains the most influential work on this topic in the Western world.

31. Common Sense
(1776) Thomas Paine

"The birthday of a new world is at hand," wrote **Thomas Paine** in a 50-page booklet that fueled the passions of American colonists.

Published anonymously in January, 1776, *Common Sense* argued that **Great Britain** was exploiting the **American colonies**, the colonists received no advantage from remaining under British domination, and that "common sense" called for them to obtain independence and establish their own government.

In dramatic rhetorical style, Paine ignited revolutionary fervor with statements such as "Government even in its best state is but a necessary evil" and "Of more worth is one honest man to society and in the sight of God, than all the crowned ruffians that ever lived."

Paine argued eloquently against the monarchy, stating, "For all men being originally equals, no one by birth could have a right to set up his own family in perpetual preference to all others forever."

More than half a million copies of *Common Sense* sold quickly—nearly one for every five colonists. Its contents were discussed in taverns and on street corners, stirring support for the on-going **Revolutionary War**.

In addition to copies sold, excerpts from *Common Sense* were published freely in every patriot newspaper, inciting the colonists to rebel against British rule.

"Without the pen of Paine, the sword of Washington would have been wielded in vain," said John Adams, who along with other founding fathers signed the **Declaration of Independence** six months after Paine published his inflammatory booklet.

Ironically, the voice of the American Revolution was born in England in 1737. He left school at 13 to work in his father's trade as a corset maker, but later ran away to become a sailor.

In 1774, Paine arrived in Philadelphia. He became editor of *Pennsylvania Magazine* and soon began publishing controversial writings anonymously, including *Common Sense*.

After the revolution, Paine was appointed secretary of the Committee of Foreign Affairs for the new American government. For the remainder of his life, he continued to publish controversial works, such as *The Rights of Man*, a criticism of monarchy written in response to Edmund Burke's attack on the French Revolution, and *The Age of Reason*, which criticized organized religion and for which Paine was roundly condemned in both England and America.

Thomas Paine

Before his death in 1809, Paine summarized the goal behind his works: "to rescue man from tyranny . . . and enable him to be free, and establish government for himself."

Advancing liberty was worth the personal sacrifices, Paine believed. "Reputation is what men and women think of us," he concluded; "Character is what God and the angels know of us."

The Federalist Papers, a series of **essays** written by three of America's **founding fathers**, helped persuade citizens in the United States of the need for a much stronger federal government, resulting in the ratification of the **U.S. Constitution**.

In the aftermath of the American Revolution, the 13-newly independent states formed a government under the **Articles of Confederation**, a document that organized a loose "league of friendship" among the member states. Under the Articles, each state retained its sovereignty, freedom, and independence; the central government consisted solely of a Congress, which was severely limited because it had no way of enforcing its authority.

Seeking to address this problem, 12 states sent delegates to a convention in Philadelphia in 1787 to revise the Articles of Confederation; instead, they drafted an entirely new document—the U.S. Constitution—and created a new frame of government.

To win support for the Constitution, two delegates to the convention—**Alexander Hamilton** from New York, and Virginia's **James Madison**, who authored much of the new document—along with attorney **John Jay**, composed a series of essays urging ratification by the states.

The three men wrote 85 essays, published in 1787 and 1788 under the name "**Publius**." Hamilton and Madison wrote the great majority of the essays, which persuasively presented arguments of the Federalists, those favoring ratification of the Constitution.

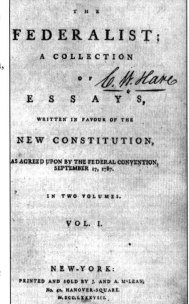

The Federalist essays demonstrated the necessity of a strong union, and the failures of the Articles of Confederation. The essays stated that the new Constitution created a republican form of government that was strong, but that was restrained by checks and balances—three branches of government: legislative, executive, and judicial.

To assure law and order, a central government was necessary, the essayists argued. Without a central government, anarchy would ensue.

Hamilton observed that the people were being asked to decide "whether societies of men are really capable or not of establishing good government from reflection and choice," and warned that a wrong decision would be considered "as the general misfortune of mankind."

The Federalist Papers were widely circulated in pamphlet form and reprinted in newspapers. Later, the collected essays were published in book form. Their widespread publication helped gather public support for ratification of the Constitution. In July 1788, the required nine states ratified the document and the new government was formed.

The Federalist Papers' influence continues to this day. When considering controversial cases, the **U.S. Supreme Court** has often referred to *The Federalist Papers* as an authoritative source for understanding the intent of the framers of the Constitution.

The Federalist Papers

33. A Vindication of the Rights of Woman
(1792) Mary Wollstonecraft

One of the earliest **feminist** documents, **Mary Wollstonecraft's** *A Vindication of the Rights of Woman* was a cry for full civil and political rights for women, including equal education and employment opportunities.

In her treatise, Wollstonecraft criticized educational limits, which kept women "in a state of ignorance and slavish dependence." She condemned marriage and decried emphasis on women's appearances: "How many women thus waste life away the prey of discontent, who might have practiced as physicians, regulated a farm, managed a shop, and stood erect, supported by their own industry, instead of hanging their heads surcharged with the dew of sensibility, that consumes the beauty to which it at first gave luster."

The first major feminine treatise was inspired after Wollstonecraft became incensed reading a pamphlet written by French statesman **Charles Talleyrand-Perigord**. Wollstone-craft dedicated her book to Talleyrand, in hopes of improving the status of women in France. In the dedication, she argued:

Mary Wollstonecraft

"I plead for my sex, not for myself . . . Who made man the exclusive judge, if woman partake with him the gift of reason? In this style, argue tyrants of every denomination . . . Do you not act a similar part, when you force all women, by denying them civil and political rights, to remain immured in their families groping in the dark?"

Omitting rights for women in France would be a tragic flaw, Wollstonecraft concluded, arguing:

". . . when your constitution is revised, the Rights of Women may be respected, if it be fully proved that reason calls for this respect, and loudly demands JUSTICE for one half of the human race."

Born in England in 1759, Wollstonecraft's views were shaped by the oppression of her mother and sister. Her father reportedly treated her mother abusively.

Wollstonecraft, her sisters, and a friend opened a school in 1784. While running the school, Wollstonecraft met a group of men known as **Rational Dissenters**, who believed that conscience and reason should be used to make moral choices.

One of the Rational Dissenters, publisher **Joseph Johnson**, commissioned Wollstonecraft to write a book, *Thoughts on the Education of Girls*. She then moved to London, where she became a contributor to a journal founded by Johnson. In 1792, she published *A Vindication of the Rights of Woman*.

In 1797, Wollstonecraft died of blood poisoning resulting from childbirth. Her daughter, Mary, became a writer in her own right, best known for authoring *Frankenstein*.

It took over a century for Wollstonecraft's ideas to gain popularity. Her writing inspired the **women's suffrage movement**, and the feminist movement, which continues striving to attain equal rights for women to this day.

Seeking to free his homeland, **Venezuela**, from Spanish control, **Simón Bolívar** escaped to **Cartagena** in New Granada (present-day Colombia) in 1812. There, he wrote the *Cartagena Manifesto*, a plea to the government of New Granada to help drive the Spanish from Venezuela. Ultimately, Bolívar's leadership banished Spanish forces throughout South America, where he became known as **"The Liberator."**

Bolívar was born in 1783 in Venezuela, a Spanish colony. He studied under tutors and continued his education in Spain, inspired by the Enlightenment authors such as Rousseau, Locke, and Voltaire.

Returning home around 1810, Bolívar was determined to free South America from European rule. In 1811, Venezuela became the first of Spain's American colonies to declare independence, but supporters of Spain's King Ferdinand overthrew the new ruling council.

Bolívar fled to Cartagena, where he issued his famous manifesto. He made an impassioned plea for a professional military and a strong central government, rather than **federalism**, (shared authority among states or provinces) to free his people from Spanish rule. For a war of independence to triumph, Bolívar was willing to sacrifice other considerations—such as popular elections and representative governments:

. . . what country in the world, however well trained and republican it may be, can, amidst internal factions and foreign war, be governed by so complicated and weak a system as the federal? . . . It is essential that a government mold itself, so to speak, to the nature and circumstances, the times, and the men that comprise it. If these factors are prosperity and peace, the government should be mild and protecting; but if they are turbulence and disaster, it should be stern and arm itself with a firmness that matches its dangers, without

Simon Bolivar

regard for laws or constitutions until happiness and peace have been reestablished."

In 1819, Bolívar defeated the Spanish in a daring military attack. He freed slaves and issued bonuses to soldiers to boost morale. A year later, he founded the **Republic of Gran Colombia**, a federation of Venezuela, Colombia, and Ecuador. He modeled the Republic's legislature after Britain's Parliament and named himself president, but drew some criticism for dictatorial tactics.

In 1824, Bolívar joined forces with military leader **Antonio Jose de Sucre** to eliminate Spain's presence in South America. The **Republic of Bolivia** was created in Bolívar's honor.

In 1829, the Republic of Gran Colombia fell apart when first Venezuela and then Ecuador seceded from the federation. Disillusioned, Bolívar resigned the presidency and left the Republic. He died of tuberculosis in 1830.

Although Bolívar's grand republic failed to survive, his vision of freedom—so eloquently expressed in the *Cartagena Manifesto*—endured, setting the stage for modern Latin American democracies.

35. Pride and Prejudice
(1813) Jane Austen

Pride and Prejudice, **Jane Austen's** highly acclaimed novel **satirizing** early 19th century **English society** and its rigid conventions, continues to be widely popular with audiences of all ages, nearly 200 years after its initial publication.

"It is a truth universally acknowledged, that a single man in possession of a good fortune must be in want of a wife," begins the novel, which describes in humorous detail the efforts of five sisters to find suitable husbands.

The story centers around Elizabeth, a witty and intelligent woman, and her romance with Fitzwilliam Darcy, a wealthy, aristocratic suitor. Pride and prejudice lead to mistaken first impressions, as he disdains courting a woman from a lower social class.

"She is tolerable; but not handsome enough to tempt me," he says upon seeing Elizabeth at a ball. Overhearing the snub, Elizabeth dismisses him as arrogant. She later rejects his marriage proposal, stunning him with scathing criticism. Ultimately, the couple learns to look beyond pretense, discovering that they are actually well-suited.

Born in 1775 at Steventon, Hampshire, England, Austen was one of eight children. Her father, a rector, could not afford to give his daughters large dowries for marriage, placing Austen in circumstances similar to her female characters.

Jane Austen

In her teens, Austen wrote humorous parodies of literary works. From 1795 to 1799, she wrote drafts of several major novels: *Sense and Sensibility, Pride and Prejudice,* and *Northanger Abbey.*

Pride and Prejudice, originally titled *First Impressions,* may have begun as an exchange of letters between Austen and her sister. The manuscript was offered to a publisher by Austen's father in 1797, but was rejected.

Sense and Sensibility was published anonymously in 1811, with authorship listed on the title page as 'By a Lady.' Popularity of the novel led to publication of *Pride and Prejudice* in 1813 credited as 'by the author of *Sense and Sensibility.'*

Although Austen's name did not appear on her novels until after her death in 1817, the "secret" of the author's identity became widely known by late 1813, when second editions of *Pride and Prejudice* and *Sense and Sensibility* were published.

Austen's works were translated into French and also sold in America during her lifetime. *Pride and Prejudice,* her most popular and widely translated work, has never gone out of print. In recent years, the story has been turned into both theatrical and television movies—in the United States as well as in England— spurring renewed interest in Austen's other works and broadening her appeal.

36. The Last of the Mohicans

(1826)   James Fenimore Cooper

The Last of the Mohicans is the most famous of the five novels known as the *Leather-Stocking Tales* by **James Fenimore Cooper**, considered by many to be America's first significant novelist.

Cooper was the first writer to create distinctly American characters, settings, and—with his frontier adventure stories—distinctly **American themes**. Cooper was also the first to evoke a tragic vision: the destruction of the American wilderness by colonists attracted to the New Eden.

In *The Last of the Mohicans*, he lamented the devastation of the **native Americans** by white settlers during the **French and Indian Wars** (1754–1761):

"The pale faces are masters of the earth, and the time of the red men has not yet come again. My day has been too long. In the morning I saw the sons of Unamis happy and strong; and yet, before the night has come, have I lived to see the last warrior of the wise race of the Mohicans."

Unlike later writers, who often stereotyped native Americans as bloodthirsty savages, Cooper imbued his Indian characters with a range of emotions. He glorified their dignity and nobility, leading some to criticize him for idealizing native American culture.

Published in 1826, the novel appeared during heated debate over efforts to remove American Indians from their native lands to a region west of the Mississippi—a movement carried out in the 1830s with tragic results. The novel became an instant best seller, establishing its author as an important American literary figure.

Born in 1789, Cooper was one of 12 children. When he was an infant, his father founded a primitive settlement on Lake Otsego in upstate New York. The setting provided Cooper with first-hand observations of frontier life, although his descriptions of native

James Fenimore Cooper

Americans were based mainly on stories told by his father.

In 1821, he published *The Spy*, a novel set during the American Revolution; it established his literary reputation.

From 1823 to 1841 he published the five novels in the *Leather-Stocking Tales*: *The Pioneers*, *The Last of the Mohicans*, *The Prairies*, *The Pathfinder*, and *The Deerslayer*. Each featured a uniquely American hero, wilderness scout **Natty Bumppo**, a frontiersman patterned partly after **Daniel Boone**. The character became the inspiration for many future homespun heroes of American fiction.

Cooper, who died in 1851, spent his final years in the settlement founded by his father, renamed **Cooperstown**. His most famous and popular work, *The Last of the Mohicans*, remains a classic tale of life in colonial America—told with a unique view of the people whose lives were forever changed by the colonial settlers.

37. Nature
(1836) Ralph Waldo Emerson

In his famous lyrical essay, *Nature,* philosopher **Ralph Waldo Emerson** founded an American branch of European Romanticism that became known as **Transcendentalism**, a movement stressing the spiritual potential of every person.

A former **Unitarian minister** who left the church to seek a more personal relationship with God, Emerson concluded that divine revelation depended upon man's relationship with **nature**. God, he came to believe, could best be found by looking into one's own soul.

In *Nature,* Emerson extolled each reader to "build your own world" by rejecting "dry bones" of the past, seeking a "religion by revelation" instead. "There are new lands, new men, new thoughts," he wrote. "Let us demand our own works and laws and worship."

Nature repudiated religion and materialism, urging readers to seek divine inspiration through the natural world. "The sun illuminates only the eye of the man, but shines into the eye and the heart of the child . . . The lover of nature is he whose inward and outward senses are still truly adjusted to each other; who has retained the spirit of infancy into the era of manhood."

Born in Boston in 1803, Emerson followed in the footsteps of his father, a minister in Puritan New England. He attended Divinity School at Harvard University, where he also gained exposure to Hindu and Buddhist philosophies.

Ralph Waldo Emerson

Around 1830, Emerson began to question religious doctrines, as well as the teachings of the rationalist philosophers who believed in mechanical explanations for everything in the universe. Instead, Emerson believed, free will could help mankind "**transcend**" the materialistic world, finding enlightenment from one's own soul and from the divine "oversoul" in all living things.

Emerson resigned from the pulpit in 1832 and went to Europe. There he met the leading writers of the **Romantic movement**, who emphasized discovery through the senses and personal experience rather than through reliance on rational thought. Before returning to America, he visited a botanical exhibition in Paris, where he resolved to become a "naturalist." His first book, published in 1836, was *Nature.* Before long it became the Bible for many readers who shared Emerson's philosophy; soon groups of people with the same strong views of the power of nature were given a name: the Transcendentalist movement. It became popular throughout the 1840s and '50s. During this period, Emerson also founded a quarterly periodical, *The Dial,* which published writings of authors who shared his philosophy.

Emerson's reputation was at its height during the years leading up to the Civil War. His words inspired a generation of Americans, and his followers became influential in both the **antislavery movement** and the emerging **women's movement**.

38. A Christmas Carol
(1843) Charles Dickens

Charles Dickens's *A Christmas Carol,* the endearing story of **Ebenezer Scrooge's** transformation from miser to benefactor, became an instant holiday classic when it was published, and inspired a new genre of literature: the **Christmas book**.

Dickens was already a famous writer when he published *A Christmas Carol,* the first of five Christmas books, in December 1843. The story describes Ebenezer Scrooge's Christmas Eve encounters with the **ghosts** of Christmas past, present, and future. Unloved as a child and abandoned to boarding school during holidays, Scrooge had grown obsessed with money and power. He was also bitter because he had lost the one woman he had ever loved. He despised Christmas, and whenever anyone mentioned the spirit of the holiday, he would exclaim with disdain, "Bah, humbug."

Through the ghosts, Scrooge learns how others view him— as a stingy, unfeeling man. He also becomes terribly frightened and upset when the ghost of Christmas future shows him that, even after he dies, no one has anything good to say about him.

As a result of his visitations, Scrooge resolves to change his life. He becomes moved by the plight of **Tiny Tim**, the ailing child of his impoverished clerk, **Bob Cratchit**. The day after Christmas, Scrooge informs Cratchit that he will be getting a raise in pay, and vows to get a good doctor for Tiny Tim. At the end of the story, Dickens describes the transformation in Scrooge.

"He became as good a friend, as good a master, and as good a man as the good old city knew, or any other good old city, town, or borough in the good old world."

The final paragraph in *A Christmas Carol* also describes Scrooge's complete change of heart regarding Christmas:

". . . and it was always said of him, that he knew how to keep Christmas well, if any man alive possessed the knowledge."

Dickens' sentimentality and belief in helping others stemmed from his own impoverished childhood. Born in 1812, at age 12 Dickens was forced to work in a factory after his parents and siblings were confined to debtors' prison. Themes from his bleak childhood later appeared in his novels, such as *Oliver Twist* and *David Copperfield.*

Over the years, *A Christmas Carol* has become a classic, performed thousands of times by theater groups around the world; the story has also been made into a motion picture several times, in England and in the United States. In addition, the name Scrooge entered the English lexicon as the definitive "stingy, miserable person," ironically, since at the story's conclusion, Scrooge has changed his ways.

Charles Dickens

39. Tales
(1845) Edgar Allan Poe

Edgar Allan Poe was a master at crafting **short stories** steeped in Gothic horror, mystery, and spine-tingling suspense. *Tales*, the first book to include all of Poe's short stories, featured his classic horror works, such as "**The Tell-Tale Heart**," "**The Cask of Amontillado**," and "**The Fall of the House of Usher**." It also included the world's first detective story, "**The Murders in the Rue Morgue**."

Originally published in 1845, *Tales* was reprinted in 1849, a year after the author's death, as part of *The Works of the Late Edgar Allan Poe*.

Poe was born in Boston in 1809 to an English actress and an American actor; he was orphaned before his third birthday. As a young man, he attended the University of Virginia, until he ran up gambling debts and began drinking heavily.

In 1839, Poe began writing tales of **supernatural horror**. In 1845, he published the first edition of his *Tales*. In these stories, Poe explored the dark side of romanticism by emphasizing sensual discovery of the **macabre**, dwelling on fear, death, insanity, revenge, and the supernatural. In some tales, he used unconventional storytellers, placing readers into the minds of murderers.

In "The Cask of Amontillado," Montresor, the narrator, lures Fortunato, a wine connoisseur afflicted with a cold, into catacombs to sample fine wine. Fortunato observes, "I shall not die of a cough." Montresor replies, "True, true."

Edgar Allan Poe

Ironically, Montresor knows that a cough will not kill Fortunato—since Montresor plans to murder him. Poe foreshadows this in revealing a crypt where the Amontillado wine is reportedly stored:

"Its walls had been lined with human remains . . . Three sides of this interior crypt were still ornamented in this manner."

Bones removed from a fourth wall lay scattered outside, revealing a recess into which Montresor lures his drunken victim. He chains Fortunato to the wall, then seals him into the tomb using mortar, stones, and a trowel.

Poe reveals Fortunato's horror through the killer's point of view. First, a "low, moaning cry" followed by "a succession of loud and shrill screams . . . from the throat of the chained [Fortunato]."

Montresor completes his act with chilling calm, sealing the last stone, then stacking the old bones against the new wall where, the narrator recalls, they have remained undisturbed for half a century.

Poe was a master at crafting eerie atmospheres, as in "The Fall of the House of Usher," in which a narrator observes vacant "eye-like" windows and perceives "a sense of insufferable gloom pervading my spirit."

Poe's psychological thrillers laid the groundwork for future creators of macabre fiction, everyone from master filmmaker **Alfred Hitchcock** to horror novelist **Stephen King**.

40. Narrative of the Life of Frederick Douglass (1845) Frederick Douglass

Born into **slavery**, **Frederick Douglass** escaped to freedom and became a powerful voice in the **abolitionist movement** to end that institution. His speeches were so eloquent that critics doubted he had ever been a slave. To dispel those doubts, Douglass wrote his autobiography.

The *Narrative of the Life of Frederick Douglass* awakened the conscience of a nation. His book exposed the horrors of slavery, adding fuel to the abolitionists' fire. **Harriet Beecher Stowe** used the *Narrative* as a resource when writing *Uncle Tom's Cabin* (see no. 45).

Born in 1817, Douglass was separated from his enslaved mother shortly after birth and sent to live with his grandmother on a Maryland plantation. At age eight, he became a house servant in Baltimore, where the owner's wife defied state law and taught Douglass how to read. Later, he continued his education in secret. Studying a book on oratory, he learned public speaking techniques and became a great orator.

Apprenticed in a shipyard, he disguised himself as a sailor and escaped to New York. In 1845, he published his *Narrative*, chilling readers with descriptions such as this recollection of a slave master:

"He was a cruel man, hardened by a long life of slaveholding. He would at times seem to take great pleasure in whipping a slave. I have often been awakened at the dawn of day by the most heartrending shrieks of an own aunt . . . whom he used to tie up to a joist, and whip upon her naked back . . . It struck me with awful force. It was the blood-stained gate, the entrance to the hell of slavery, through which I was about to pass."

Douglass named his former owners and described in detail his life in bondage. He revealed his fear of **fugitive slave hunters**, whom he likened to "ferocious beasts of the forest" who "lie in wait for their prey."

Frederick Douglass

Douglass omitted details of his escape, however, to protect slaves who might follow his path to freedom.

He recalled amazement upon visiting wharves in New Bedford, where he witnessed free men at work: "I heard no deep oaths or horrid curses on the laborer. I saw no whipping of men . . . Every man appeared to understand his work, and went at it with a sober, yet cheerful earnestness, which betokened . . . a sense of his own dignity as a man."

After publishing his *Narrative*, Douglass feared capture under fugitive slave laws. He went to Europe, but later returned when friends purchased his freedom.

He died in 1885; his stirring autobiography remains a legacy of the struggle to win freedom for his people.

41. Wuthering Heights
(1847) Emily Brontë

Wuthering Heights, **Emily Brontë's** passionate novel of love, hatred and revenge in the **English moors**, has become a literary classic, considered by some critics to be among the finest novels in the English language.

The novel has an unusual structure, told through viewpoints of **two narrators**—a servant and a tenant. The story spans two generations, recounting the tragic impact of the adopted waif, **Heathcliff**, on two families.

Emily Brontë

Wuthering Heights revolves around the tumultuous relationship between Heathcliff and **Catherine**. After Catherine is forced to marry another man, the brooding Heathcliff feels betrayed. When Catherine, on her deathbed, confesses her love and selfishly wishes that they could be together in death, an embittered Heathcliff responds first with cruelty, "Why did you betray your own heart, Cathy? . . .You deserve this." On reflection, his anger turns to anguish, "Do I want to live?"

Catherine's death leaves Heathcliff embittered, vowing revenge upon the families. His violent obsession evolves into apparent madness as he is haunted by Catherine's ghost. After Heathcliff's death years later, however, witnesses avow that two spirits wander the misty moors together, in eternity.

The novel was poorly received when it was published in 1847. Critics found it too savage and depressing. Readers, expecting a comedy of manners similar to **Jane Austen's** books, were disappointed by the novel's somber tone and emotional intensity.

However, over time literary experts have come to appreciate the work. Noted author **Joyce Carol Oates** believes the novel's power was not understood by 19th century readers, but noted, "it can be seen by us . . . as brilliantly of that time—and contemporaneous with our own."

Daughter of an English clergyman, Emily Brontë was born in 1818 in an isolated rectory on the Yorkshire moors where she spent nearly all of her life.

As a young girl, Emily and three of her sisters attended the Clergy Daughters' School. The infamous institution was later depicted in *Jane Eyre* (1847), a novel written by **Charlotte Brontë**, Emily's sister.

After the deaths of Emily's two older sisters, she and Charlotte returned home to live with their remaining siblings, sister Anne and brother Branwell. The Brontë sisters spent many hours inventing imaginary kingdoms and writing about their adventures. In 1846, Emily and her sisters published a book of poetry under assumed names. A year later, *Wuthering Heights* was published.

After the death of her brother in September 1848, Emily's own health began to deteriorate. She died that December from a cold that spread to her lungs. *Wuthering Heights* was her only novel.

42. Civil Disobedience
(1849) Henry David Thoreau

"Unjust laws exist; shall we be content to obey them, or shall we endeavor to amend them, . . .or shall we transgress them at once?" **Henry David Thoreau** asked readers that question in one of the most important **political essays** ever written. When an unjust law requires a person to commit injustice upon another, he concluded, "then I say, break the law."

Civil Disobedience was written after Thoreau spent a night in jail for refusing to pay a poll tax. He wrote the essay to explain that his conscience would not allow him to pay a tax to the government, since the money would be used to support causes he did not believe in, such as enforcing slavery laws and financing the Mexican-American war.

Believing "that government is best which governs least," Thoreau argued that **individual rights** must take precedence over state authority, and that individuals should protest injustice.

"Under a government which imprisons any unjustly, the true place for a just man is also in prison . . ." he wrote.

He also asserted that individuals acting collectively can bring about change:

"A minority is powerless while it conforms to the majority . . . but it is irresistible when it clogs by its whole weight. If the alternative is to keep all just men in prison, or give up war and slavery, the State will not hesitate which to choose. If a thousand men were not to pay their tax-bills this year, that would not be a violent and bloody measure, as it would be to pay them, and enable the State to commit violence and shed innocent blood. This is, in fact, the definition of a peaceable revolution . . ."

Thoreau was born in 1817 in Concord, Massachusetts. He graduated from Harvard and became a teacher, but later returned to Concord.

Thoreau loved the outdoors, and he built a cabin on land his friend **Ralph Waldo Emerson** owned at **Walden Pond** on the outskirts of town. Thoreau lived there from 1845 to 1847, writing and reflecting on nature. In 1849, he published *Civil Disobedience*. In 1854, he published another landmark work, *Walden, or Life in the Woods*, celebrating nature.

Henry David Thoreau

Thoreau's advocacy of civil disobedience had a long-lasting impact. His message profoundly influenced future leaders, affecting the course of history more than a century later.

During the 1930s and 40s, **Mohandas Gandhi** used **nonviolent resistance** to protest British imperialism in India; and in the 1950s and '60s, civil rights leader **Martin Luther King, Jr.** followed Thoreau's policy of passive resistance to help end racial segregation in the United States.

43. David Copperfield
(1849-1850) Charles Dickens

In *David Copperfield*, **Charles Dickens** drew on his own **tragic childhood** to create an indelible portrait of the ordeals faced by orphaned or abandoned children, as well as the dismal **social conditions of mid-19th century England**.

Filled with the author's customary mix of colorful, unforgettable characters, *David Copperfield* tells the story of a young boy, mistreated by his stepfather, orphaned by the death of his mother, forced to endure poverty and hardship, and then redeemed by the love of a devoted young woman.

The fictional waif, Copperfield, shares much in common with the author. Both suffered abandonment by parents. Dickens, like Copperfield, was forced as a child to work in a waterfront warehouse affixing labels to liquor bottles—a nightmare that haunted him all of his life. Both suffered betrayals of trust and saw an important adult figure imprisoned for debt. Both also triumphed over adversity, becoming successful writers.

An illustration from *David Copperfield*

Copperfield's recollection of the waterfront warehouse carries a chilling ring of autobiographical truth:

". . . the squeaking and scuffling of the old grey rats down in the cellars; and the dirt and rottenness of the place; are things, not of man years ago, in my mind, but of the present instant."

Working amid ragtag boys from rough backgrounds, Copperfield suffered disillusionment:

" [I] felt my hopes of growing up to be a learned and distinguished man, crushed . . . I mingled my tears with the water in which I was washing the bottles . . ."

Though shamed by his ordeal, Copperfield, like Dickens, also took pride in rising above his circumstances:

". . .but for the mercy of God, I might easily have been, for all the care that was taken of me, a little robber or a little vagabond."

Born in 1812, Charles Dickens was one of eight children. After his father was sent to debtor's prison, his mother took the other children to live at the prison, but forced young Charles to work at a warehouse.

He had little schooling, but taught himself shorthand and became a parliamentary reporter. Serial publication of *The Pickwick Papers* made Dickens a literary celebrity at age 25.

David Copperfield was published serially in 1849 and 1850 in periodicals, and in 1850, in book form. Dickens wrote several other notable works before his death in 1870.

In *David Copperfield*, as well as in his other major novels, Dickens addressed not merely the misfortunes of children, but the prospect of rescue through intervention of good-hearted people and a character's own strength of will. Through most of his works, Dickens offered readers an enduring legacy of hope.

44. The Scarlet Letter
(1850) Nathaniel Hawthorne

Sin, punishment, and atonement emerge as central themes in *The Scarlet Letter*, the acclaimed novel by American author **Nathaniel Hawthorne**.

Set in **Puritan New England** during the 17th century, *The Scarlet Letter* centers around **Hester Prynne**, a young woman who becomes pregnant after her husband has abandoned her. Condemned as an adulteress, she is forced to wear a red letter "A" as punishment for her shame. Despite enormous pressure, she refuses to name her lover. Her sin is contrasted against the purity of the offspring of her illicit affair, her child, **Pearl**.

Hester's husband, **Roger Chillingworth**, returns and becomes obsessed with his quest to expose his wife's lover and exact vengeance. Consumed by guilt, the **Reverend Dimmesdale** at last comes forward to confess his sin:

"He turned towards the scaffold, and stretched forth his arms. 'Hester," said he, 'come hither! Come, my little Pearl!'"

As Dimmesdale acknowledges and embraces his daughter, Hawthorne contrasts the loving "sinner" against Hester's vindictive yet righteous husband:

" . . . old Roger Chillingworth thrust himself through the crowd, or perhaps, so dark, disturbed, and evil was his look, he rose up out of some nether region. . ."

Hawthorne shared a deep sense of morality with his Puritan ancestors, but rejected the concept of predestination. Instead, he believed redemption could be attained through love and atonement, and that the greatest sin against humanity is pride. A master of **symbolism** and **allegory**, Hawthorne also displayed powerful psychological insight into guilt as a motivator, as he probed the complexities of human choices.

Hawthorne characterized the novel as a romance, a genre which freed him from reality to use allegories and symbolism signifying his characters' passions and anxieties, reflecting the ambivalence of America's Puritan heritage.

Hawthorne was born in 1804 in Salem, Massachusetts, a town notorious for Puritan-led persecutions and witch trials during the 1690s. After graduating from Bowdoin College, he began writing short stories and articles on the moral impact of Puritanism on colonial New England.

Hawthorne went to work in 1839 at a Boston custom house. In 1841, he moved to a transcendentalist community, Brooke Farm, and published *Twice Told Tales*. He married in 1842 and moved to Concord, where he published additional works.

To support his family, Hawthorne gained an appointment as a surveyor in Salem. Poring through old documents at the custom house, he found materials about harsh punishments during the Puritan colonial era, inspiring *The Scarlet Letter*, which was published in 1850.

Acclaimed by critics even in Hawthorne's day, *The Scarlet Letter* retains its reputation as one of the finest novels ever written by an American author.

Nathaniel Hawthorne

45. Uncle Tom's Cabin
(1851-1852)   Harriet Beecher Stowe

Uncle Tom's Cabin, **Harriet Beecher Stowe's** novel exposing the horrors of **slavery,** fueled the fervor of abolitionists and helped to ignite the **Civil War.**

Uncle Tom, a slave, has been devoted to his master since childhood. When the debt-ridden master is forced to sell Tom and a small boy named **Harry**, Tom refuses a chance to escape out of loyalty to his master. To avoid separation, Harry's mother takes him and flees to the North. There, she

Uncle Tom's Cabin

persuades a senator to change his convictions about fugitive slave laws. The senator's wife also takes a stand, resolving:

"I don't know anything about politics, but I can read my Bible; and there I see that I must feed the hungry, clothe the naked, and comfort the desolate."

On a boat to New Orleans, Tom saves the life of **Eva St. Clare**, a child who convinces her father to buy Tom. Later, Tom is sold to the evil **Simon Legree**. He tries in vain to please his new master, but when Legree orders Tom to beat another slave, Tom refuses, and is beaten until he faints. Despite his suffering, Tom reveals his devotion to a higher power:

"I will hold on to the Lord, and put his commands before all . . . I'd as soon die as not. Ye may whip me, starve me, burn me— it'll only send me sooner where I want to go."

First published serially in a Washington newspaper in 1851, the novel appeared in

book form in 1852. Reviled in the South, *Uncle Tom's Cabin* was immensely popular elsewhere. Within two years, more than two million copies had been sold. It was translated into 23 languages and made into a play, which moved audiences to tears.

A clergyman's daughter born in Connecticut in 1811, Stowe attended a seminary school for girls. In 1832, her father moved the family to Cincinnati, Ohio. There, Stowe met fugitive slaves and taught former slave children at a school run by her family.

She published her first story in a magazine at age 23. Two years later, she married a clergyman and seminary professor. In 1850, she and her family moved to Maine. The same year, Congress passed the **Fugitive Slave Act**, which prohibited citizens from helping escaped slaves.

Outraged to hear otherwise good people debating whether to obey the controversial law, Stowe wrote *Uncle Tom's Cabin*. Before its publication, many Northerners shared Southerners' belief that slaves were merely property. In *Uncle Tom's Cabin*, however, Stowe portrayed slaves as human beings with heartfelt emotions.

Stowe died in 1896, after seeing her dream to abolish slavery fulfilled. *Uncle Tom's Cabin* remains one of the most influential works of fiction in American history.

46. Moby Dick
(1851) Herman Melville

Acclaimed by many critics as the Great American Novel, **Herman Melville's** *Moby Dick* recounts **Captain Ahab's** obsessive pursuit of a **white whale**. Ahab's tragic quest has been likened to Job's search for justice, Oedipus's journey for truth, and Faust's pact with the devil.

"Call me Ishmael," begins the novel, narrated by a seaman on Ahab's doomed ship. As the epic progresses, Ahab struggles with virtuous and murderous impulses, illustrating the importance of free will as opposed to predestination.

Melville probed ambiguities of goodness and evil. Ahab views the whale as a creature from hell. The book's climactic passage describes the wounded behemoth as "possessed by all the angels that fell from heaven."

Ahab's chase after Moby Dick symbolizes a conflict between the eternal forces of nature versus man. Ultimately, however, Ahab's obsession results in self-destruction. As his ship sinks, Ahab's murderous rage consumes him:

" . . . thou all-destroying but unconquering whale; to the last I grapple with thee; from hell's heart I stab at thee. . . ."

Melville's powerful **psychological and metaphysical themes** were ahead of his time, foreshadowing 20th century literary developments.

Born in New York City in 1819, Melville entered the seafaring life in his 20s, sailing for the South Seas aboard a whaler. His seagoing experiences became the subjects of his first two novels, *Typee* (1846) and *Omoo* (1847).

In creating *Moby Dick*, Melville was influenced by **Nathaniel Hawthorne's** *The Scarlet Letter*, which explored the nature of good and evil. Owners of neighboring farms, the two authors became close friends.

Melville delayed submission of his next manuscript, originally titled *The Whale*.

Inspired by Hawthorne, he altered the original light-hearted whaling adventure into a dramatic epic probing defeats and triumphs of the human spirit.

Written as the golden age of whaling was drawing to a close, *Moby Dick* was based on the myth of a white whale, a superstition in whaling lore. The darkly tragic sea yarn was "cooked in hellfire," Hawthorne confided to Melville.

Published in 1851 in England and America, *Moby Dick* was a commercial failure. Melville became a recluse, leading friends to fear for his sanity. After his next book faltered, his literary career lay in ruins.

Herman Melville

Melville died, nearly forgotten, in 1891. His final novel, *Billy Budd*, remained unpublished until 1924.

Melville's literary reputation suffered neglect until the 1920s, when **Carl Van Doren**, literary critic and editor of *The Nation*, authored *The American Novel*. Van Doren praised Melville as one of the most significant American authors and named *Moby Dick* as one of "the greatest sea romances in the whole literature of the world." Thus, Melville's literary genius was recognized and his immortality assured.

47. On the Origin of Species

(1859)   Charles Darwin

On the Origin of Species, which presented **Charles Darwin's theory of evolution**, has been called "the book that shook the world."

After observing plants and animals during a five-year voyage around the world, Darwin concluded that organisms evolve gradually through **natural selection**. Small mutations enable creatures best adapted to their environments to survive and pass along advantageous traits to their offspring. Over many generations, such changes give rise to new species, according to Darwin.

Charles Darwin

His theories, particularly his later suggestion that man descended from apes, created a storm of controversy. Just as Copernicus and Galileo upset mankind's geocentric view of the universe, so Darwin generated heated debate by questioning the origin of the human species, casting doubt on the Biblical story of **creation**. The ensuing clash between religion and science continues to this day.

Darwin was born in Shrewsbury, England in 1809. While studying at the University of Cambridge in 1831, he was influenced by a professor to sign on as an unpaid naturalist aboard the English survey ship, HMS *Beagle*. Darwin embarked on a global scientific expedition, collecting and observing plants, animals, and fossils.

During a five-week stay on the **Galapagos Islands** off Ecuador, he observed that each of the islands had separate yet similar species. Each type of finch, for example, had a different beak adapted to food sources on its island. Darwin concluded that these distinct species were related, each evolved to suit a specific environment.

Returning to England, Darwin recorded his ideas and published some of his findings in his book *A Naturalist's Voyage* (1839). He then spent the next 20 years perfecting his theories.

In 1858, Darwin's theories were presented at a London scientific meeting. A year later, he published *On the Origin of Species*, which sold out on the first day. Within one year, many supporters called the book the leading work in natural philosophy in the history of mankind.

Yet, the book provoked criticism from some scientists and many religious opponents. Opposition intensified in 1871 with publication of Darwin's *The Descent of Man*, in which he theorized that man had descended from an earlier, subhuman form. Until his death in 1882, Darwin was both praised and vilified for his theories.

Scientists have since validated many of Darwin's beliefs. Discoveries in genetics reveal how traits are passed through genes to future generations. Molecular biology enables comparison of genetic structures from different species, while fossil-dating techniques identify when ancient species lived.

While evolution theory has gained widespread acceptance among scientists, religious debate continues to rage, and the public remains divided in its belief of Darwin's theory."

48. Alice's Adventures in Wonderland
(1865) Lewis Carroll

Lewis Carroll artfully contrasts absurdity and logic in his fantasy tale, *Alice's Adventures in Wonderland*. A classic in children's literature, the work also contains amusing overtones of **social satire**, assuring its appeal to readers of all ages.

In the whimsical story, a little girl named Alice falls down a well into a strange land where everything occurs with a fantastic illogicality. She finds that she can become a giantess or a pygmy by chewing on different sides of a magic mushroom. She also has a series of remarkable adventures with a variety of colorful characters—among them, the **White Rabbit**, the **Cheshire Cat**, the **Mock Turtle**, and the **Queen of Hearts**.

"Curiouser and curiouser," cries Alice, aptly describing a world in which nothing is quite as it seems. For example, she comes across a very "curious": croquet game:

" . . . the croquet balls were live hedgehogs, and the mallets live flamingoes, and the soldiers had to double themselves up and stand on their hands and feet, to make the arches . . ."

Carroll pokes fun of the Victorian emphasis on logic, reason, and truth. In his story, reality means something different for each person—and even for the same person at different stages in life. As Alice grows up, her belief in fantasy diminishes.

Lewis Carroll is the pen name of **Charles Lutwidge Dodgson**, born in 1832, the son of a parson in the Anglican Church. As a young boy, he enjoyed writing poetry and stories to entertain his friends and siblings.

Dodgson later became a mathematician and authored several mathematical treatises. A shy individual who stammered, Dodgson was most comfortable in the company of children. He often amused them with games, puzzles, and his storytelling. It was for one of these children—young **Alice Liddell**, the daughter of a family friend—that he wrote his famous story.

Dodgson arranged for Clarendon Press to publish *Alice's Adventures in Wonderland* in 1865 under his pseudonym. Within a year, 5,000 illustrated copies had been sold. Publication of a sequel, *Through the Looking Glass and What Alice Found There* (1871) assured Carroll's fame.

In addition to its appeal to children, over the years, *Alice's Adventures in Wonderland* and its sequel became highly popular among adult readers. Advocates of the 20th century movement in art and literature called **surrealism**—which stressed the subconscious significance of imagery—believed Carroll's works displayed early examples of their principles.

Whatever the audience— young or old, girl or boy—Carroll's whimsical story and assortment of characters have continued to delight readers more than a century after the book's first publication.

An illustration of Alice at the Mad Tea Party

49. Das Kapital
(1867) Karl Marx

Das Kapital, **Karl Marx's** landmark economic work condemning capitalism, became known as the "**Bible of the working class**." The extremely influential work spurred the rise of **socialism** and **communism**, political systems based on collective ownership of the means of production.

Karl Marx

In *Das Kapital*, Marx argued that capitalists, or the **bourgeoisie**, exploited the working class, or **proletariat**. Marx maintained that capitalists exploited laborers by requiring them to work long hours for low wages, resulting in surplus profits pocketed by the capitalists. As industrialization lured capitalists to replace workers with machinery, Marx believed, high costs of machinery would lead to reduced profits and cutbacks would spark rebellion by workers.

Ultimately, Marx predicted, "the capitalist class becomes unfit to rule, because it is incompetent to assure an existence to its slave within his slavery." Capitalism would collapse, replaced by a classless society in which the working class inherits the power. Means of production would be owned by the community; individuals would contribute efforts and share in the wealth.

Volume I of *Das Kapital* was published in 1867; second and third volumes were published posthumously in 1885 and 1894, edited by Marx's collaborator, **Friedrich Engels**.

Born in Prussia (present-day Germany) in 1818, Marx studied law at the University of Bonn and later attended the University of Berlin. He became a journalist and an editor of a liberal newspaper, until his controversial articles caused the German government to close the publication.

Marx moved to France, where in 1844 he met Friedrich Engels. They formed a lifelong collaboration to organize an international working-class movement based on Communist beliefs.

Marx moved to Brussels and formed a group that became the **Communist League**. Asked to draft a statement of principles for the League, Marx and Engels wrote *The Communist Manifesto*, a pamphlet of principles later expanded in *Das Kapital*.

Marx's theories came to be known as **Marxism**, an extremely influential body of political thought. Marx's ideas were adopted by **Vladimir Lenin**, who led a workers' takeover of Russia in 1917 and created the Communist government of the **Soviet Union**. Communism also spread in the 20th century throughout Eastern Europe, South America, Asia, and Africa.

The idealistic society Marx envisioned failed to materialize, however, as oppression continued under Marxist regimes. By the early 1990s, collapse of the Soviet Communist party led to break-up of the Soviet Union and the toppling of Communist governments in Eastern Europe.

Although Communism as a world force has dramatically diminished, the theories Marx expressed in *Das Kapital* will have a lasting impact on world history.

50. Little Women
(1868)   Louisa May Alcott

Little Women, **Louisa May Alcott's** novel about four sisters growing up in New England during the **Civil War**, is one of the most popular **coming-of-age novels** for girls in American literary history.

The novel centers around the four **March sisters**—Meg, Jo, Beth, and Amy. While their father is away fighting in the Civil War, the girls learn to overcome hardships as they strive to achieve their dreams, or "castles in the air."

The story combines elements of a traditional conduct books for girls with a fictional plot. Through their mother **Marmee**, the girls learn conventional values. When Meg marries, for example, Marmee advises, "You are the sunshine-maker of the family, and if you get dismal there is no fair weather. . ."

In Jo March, however, Alcott created an untraditional female character. Jo March was the first juvenile heroine in American fiction to pursue a career dream in an era when women were expected to be solely "mothers and homemakers."

Jo vowed, "I want to do something splendid before I go into my castle—something heroic or wonderful that won't be forgotten . . . I mean to astonish you all someday. I think I shall write books and get rich and famous."

As the girls mature, they must cope with love, loss, and sacrifice. When the family endures financial hard times, Jo cuts her hair and sells it to a wigmaker. Her most poignant loss, however, occurs when Beth falls gravely ill. "Beth is my conscience, and I can't give her up; I can't!" Jo laments.

Although Jo sacrifices her writing dreams when she raises a family of her own, Alcott leaves the door open for Jo to "write a good book yet."

Little Women, though fictional, is largely autobiographical. Born in Pennsylvania in 1832, Alcott was one of four sisters who inspired the characters in *Little Women*. When her family suffered financial hardships, Louisa vowed to help through writing. She wrote sensationalized novels under a pen name, keeping her work secret.

Alcott became a teacher, and in 1852, she submitted a story under her own name to a publisher. "Stick to your teaching, Miss Alcott," he replied in one of literary history's most notorious misjudgments. "You can't write."

During the Civil War, Alcott worked as a nurse in a Washington, D.C. hospital. In 1863, *Hospital Sketches*, a book based on her wartime experiences, brought her literary success.

In 1864, her publisher asked her to write a book containing values for girls. Alcott spent eight months writing *Little Women*, which proved an instant success. More than 130 years after its publication, it remains a young adult classic.

Louisa May Alcott

51. Twenty Thousand Leagues Under the Sea (1870) Jules Verne

Known as the father of science fiction, French author **Jules Verne** foresaw many scientific advances of the 20th century, some of which he predicted in his classic **sea-adventure** novel, *Twenty Thousand Leagues Under the Sea*.

In this thrilling tale, Verne relates the fictitious story of **Captain Nemo** and the crew of the *Nautilus*, an atomic submarine. Written long before submarines or atomic energy were proven feasible, the novel describes the *Nautilus* and its undersea explorations—including visits to the South Pole and the lost city of Atlantis—in seemingly accurate detail. The book also entertains readers with vivid descriptions of perils encountered by the *Nautilus* and its crew, such as when the submarine is attacked by a giant squid.

Opposed to war, Captain Nemo attacks and destroys war ships using his submarine, which is disguised as a large sea creature equipped with a metal fin on top. Sea-going vessels initially report sightings of the mysterious attacker, described as "a long spindle-shaped object, which sometimes appeared phosphorescent and was infinitely larger and quicker than a whale."

After the loss of 200 ships is attributed to "the monster," tension rises. "Because . . . travel between the various continents was becoming increasingly dangerous, the public spoke its mind and categorically demanded that the oceans be finally rid of this formidable cetacean, whatever the cost."

At the end of the story, Captain Nemo takes his submarine into an area of the ocean known as **"The Maelstrom,"** a whirlpool that takes ships to the bottom of the sea. The novel ends with the fate of the *Nautilus* uncertain—did she escape The Maelstrom, or did Captain Nemo intentionally plan to destroy his ship because he regretted the destruction he had caused? The author says that "only the sea can answer these questions; the sea and only the sea."

Born in 1828 in Nantes, France, Jules Verne was the oldest of five children. He studied law, but decided to pursue a career in writing instead.

In addition to *Twenty Thousand Leagues Under the Sea*, Verne wrote several other tales combining fantasy and adventure to portray imagined scientific wonders. Among his most popular works were *A Journey to the Center of the Earth* (1864) and *From the Earth to the Moon* (1865). In 1873-75, his major works were translated into English, broadening his popularity.

Twenty Thousand Leagues Under the Sea helped established the **science fiction** genre. This futuristic novel, as well as Verne's other writings, inspired many young readers, including some who later attained great scientific achievements. Among them were submarine designer **Simon Lake** and **Guglielmo Marconi**, inventor of the wireless telegraph.

Jules Verne

58

52. The Brothers Karamazov
(1879-1880)   Fyodor Dostoevsky

Russian novelist **Fyodor Dostoevsky's** probing psychological intensity profoundly affected 20th century literary development. *The Brothers Karamazov* is considered by many critics to be his greatest work.

As in many of his other books, in *The Brothers Karamazov* Dostoevsky focuses on **theological and philosophical themes**: the causes of evil, the desire for faith, and the nature of freedom. The novel explores challenges to faith faced by three brothers—**Dmitry**, **Ivan**, and **Alyosha**—following the murder of their father by a fourth and illegitimate son, Smerdyakov.

Dmitry suffers anguish after he is falsely accused of the crime. Alyosha turns to faith. The intellectual Ivan, by contrast, shuns a world in which innocents, such as children, are allowed to suffer.

Ivan reveals his sentiments in a poem titled "**The Grand Inquisitor**." In the poem, Christ returns to earth during the Spanish Inquisition and is arrested as a heretic. In a scene that ranks among the most famous in Western literature, the Inquisitor explains that the Church has rejected Christ for offering people freedom—when in fact people would rather have security than free choice. To ensure happiness, the Church has built a society based on "miracle, mystery and authority," explains the Inquisitor, who represents both socialism and the Church. Paradoxically, Dostoevsky raises strong arguments against the existence of God—then refutes them to defend Christianity. Dostoevsky also suggests that tyrants, including the Inquisitor, are in fact in league with the Devil.

Ivan, descending into madness, is visited by Satan, who defends materialism. Dostoevsky's image of a "petty demon" proved highly influential on later 20th century literature and thought.

Dostoevky's grasp of psychological motivations stems from his own life, scarred by tragedies and suffering. Born in Moscow in 1821, he began his career as a writer while in his twenties. In 1846, his first novel, *Poor People*, received literary praise.

In 1849, Dostoevsky was arrested as a political radical and condemned to death. Just before his execution, his sentence was commuted to imprisonment. The mock execution proved part of his punishment—a psychological torture that profoundly influenced Dostoevsky. He endured four years in a Siberian prison camp, suffering epileptic seizures.

After ten years abroad, he returned to Russia and resumed his writing career. In 1866, he published *Crime and Punishment*, a psychological novel featuring a young murderer haunted by guilt. Despite illness and other personal problems, Dostoevsky continued to write. *The Brothers Karamazov*, his final novel, was published in 1879-1880.

Dostoevsky ranks among the greatest of all novelists. Works such as *The Brothers Karamazov* influenced 20th century existentialist authors, such as **Jean-Paul Sartre**, who stressed the importance of individual existence and freedom of choice.

Fyodor Dostoevsky

53. Treasure Island

(1883) Robert Louis Stevenson

Robert Louis Stevenson

The first and most famous novel by Scottish author **Robert Louis Stevenson**, *Treasure Island* has become a classic of children's literature and one of the world's most beloved adventure stories.

Stevenson, a master storyteller, wove a suspenseful tale of a search for buried treasure. It is narrated by **Jim Hawkins**, a boy whose adventure begins at his father's inn, following a visit from an aging seaman:

"I remember him as if it were yesterday, as he came plodding to the inn door, his sea-chest following behind him in a hand-barrow—a tall, strong, heavy, nut-brown man, his tarry pigtail falling over the shoulder of his soiled blue coat . . . and the sabre cut across one cheek . . ."

After Jim learns of the whereabouts of the buried treasure from the old sailor's papers, he enlists the help of a local doctor and a wealthy squire. They secure a ship, hire a crew, and set out to find Treasure Island. Among the ship's crew are the devious **Long John Silver** and his followers, who are out to take the treasure for themselves. As the story unfolds, young Jim foils Silver's plans, and along with his cohorts, he successfully reaches the island and finds the treasure.

The book combines a fast-paced plot with colorful characters. On one level, the novel is an entertaining tale. On a deeper level, it explores the nature of goodness, evil, and criminality. Long John Silver, the genial yet murderous pirate captain, alternately fascinates and repels, leading readers to question what compels a person to commit evil actions.

Born in Edinburgh, Scotland in 1850, Robert Louis Stevenson was frequently ill as a child. Taking refuge in his fertile imagination, he began writing poetry and prose. At the age of 21, he decided to make writing his profession.

As an adult, Stevenson suffered from tuberculosis, and spent much of his life in regions with warm climates, seeking relief from the crippling lung disease. He published travel pieces, essays, and a short story before traveling to California in 1879.

After he and his American wife returned to Scotland, he began writing *Treasure Island,* which started as a game with his stepson. *Treasure Island* was published serially in 1882, and in book form in 1883. Stevenson's success was assured three years later, with publication of both *Kidnapped* and *The Strange Case of Dr. Jekyll and Mr. Hyde.*

By the early 20th century, *Treasure Island* had become a classic, read by youngsters all over the world. Over the years, it has been turned into a motion picture on several occasions, both in England and the United States.

54. The Adventures of Huckleberry Finn
(1884) Mark Twain

"All modern American literature comes from one book by **Mark Twain** called *Huckleberry Finn*," novelist Ernest Hemingway once wrote. Although that may be a slight exaggeration, there is no question that the novel has significantly influenced the development of American fiction.

Set around the 1840s, the story relates the exploits of young **Huck Finn**, a character Twain introduced in his earlier novel, *The Adventures of Tom Sawyer* (1876). After he runs away from his brutal father, Huck meets **Jim**, an escaped slave. Together, they flee aboard a raft on the **Mississippi River**.

On their lengthy journey downstream, they make occasional stops in the towns along the banks, and come across various segments of society, including con men, traveling actors, thieves, and southern gentility. Through these encounters, Twain captures a multitude of dialects and human activities, as well as the rhythms, sights, and sounds that existed in **pre-Civil War** mid-America.

As he becomes friends with Jim, Huck wrestles with his conscience, knowing it is illegal to help a slave escape. He considers turning Jim in, but as Huck gets to know him, he learns about the dignity and worth of human life. Instead, when Jim is recaptured, Huck helps him escape. In the end, it turns out that Jim had been freed earlier by his owner just before she died. Huck decides again to head out for new lands because he does not like "civilized society."

The story is told in a first person narrative, and Huck spins the tale using colorful slang language. Twain's irreverent humor overlies a deeper message. Although the novel has been criticized—and banned—for its racial language and overtones, it reveals Twain's commitment to freedom, and reflects ambivalent attitudes towards slavery prevalent along the Mississippi River during the author's boyhood.

Mark Twain

Mark Twain was born **Samuel Langhorne Clemens**, in 1835 in Florida, Missouri. As a youth he traveled and worked as a newspaper apprentice; at 23, he became a riverboat pilot on the Mississippi River. During the Civil War, Clemens headed west to mining camps in Nevada and California. Soon, he began signing newspaper articles as Mark Twain. Publication of "The Celebrated Jumping Frog of Calaveras County," an amusing tale reprinted in many newspapers, assured his fame as a writer.

When *The Adventures of Huckleberry Finn* was published, it provoked instant controversy. Some critics praised the work; others condemned it. However, it proved immensely popular with readers.

Twain's wry humor, use of colloquial language, and portrayal of American themes gave rise to a uniquely American style of literature, which has influenced authors as diverse as **Ernest Hemingway** and **William Faulkner**.

55. War and Peace
(1886)   Leo Tolstoy

War and Peace, Russian author **Leo Tolstoy's** sweeping saga set during the **Napoleonic Wars**, is considered by many literary experts to be the greatest novel ever written. Its realism, breadth of scope, and penetrating psychological depth remain unparalleled.

The novel, which took Tolstoy seven years to write, spans the years 1805 to 1820, encompassing events before and after Napoleon's invasion of Russia. The work contrasts the everyday lives of upper class families against hardships endured by the nation, ridiculing the upper class's self-centered attitudes.

In the book's opening scene, for example, **Anna Pavlovna**, a lady of the Empress's court, says to **Prince Vassily**, "I confess that all these festivities and fireworks are beginning to pall."

Tolstoy revealed the character's shallow nature:

"The affected smile which played continually about Anna Pavlovna's face, out of keeping as it was with her faded looks, expressed a spoilt child's continued consciousness of a charming failing of which she had neither the wish nor the power to correct herself. . ."

By contrast, Tolstoy vividly described the consequences of combat on the common man. At a hospital, he depicts an old soldier with a face "thin as a skeleton's" propping up a "young soldier with a waxen pallor on his snub-nosed and still freckled face." Informing a visiting aristocrat that the soldier has been dead since morning, the old man adds, "We've begged and begged, your honour . . . We're men too, not dogs."

Tolstoy drew controversy for his theories on war and those who wage it. He criticized historians' tendency to credit major deeds to a single heroic individual.

In *War and Peace*, Tolstoy portrayed the conflict's unsung heroes, humanized soldiers on both sides, and questioned the validity of war. After the character **Rostov** receives a medal for accepting the surrender of a terrified young officer he'd nearly killed, he ponders, "Is this, then, all that is meant by heroism?"

Son of a wealthy Russian nobleman, Tolstoy was born in 1828 near Moscow. As a young man, he joined the army and fought in the Crimean War, where he gained respect for the heroism of common soldiers.

Tolstoy married and had 13 children. He managed his estate while working on his two masterpieces. *War and Peace*, written in the 1860s, wasn't published until 1886. *Anna Karenina* was completed in the 1870s.

In his later years, Tolstoy rejected his life of wealth. He gave up material possessions, and began writing religious works. He died in 1910.

In its scope, literary style, and historical content, *War and Peace* is considered a monumental achievement by one of the world's greatest novelists.

Tolstoy

56. A Study in Scarlet
(1887) Sir Arthur Conan Doyle

In *A Study in Scarlet*, author **Sir Arthur Conan Doyle** introduced to the world **Sherlock Holmes**, the fictitious detective who has become one of the most enduring characters in English literature.

Born in Scotland in 1859, Arthur Conan Doyle, took up writing to pay his medical school expenses. After graduating from the University of Edinburgh, he became an optician. In his spare time, he created Sherlock Holmes, a character based on one of Doyle's professors.

First published in 1887, *A Study in Scarlet* proved immediately popular. Readers were fascinated by Holmes's brilliant powers of deductive reasoning and eccentric traits—playing the violin, fencing, smoking a Meerschaum pipe, and wearing deerstalker attire.

Holmes uses virtually impossible-to-discern clues to solve baffling mysteries. His remarkable deductive ability was based in part on his keen observation of detail, as the master sleuth describes:

"By a man's finger-nails, by his coat-sleeve, by his boots, by his trouser-knees, by the callosities of his forefinger and thumb, by his expression . . . by each of these things a man's calling is plainly revealed. That all united should fail to enlighten the competent inquirer in any case is almost inconceivable."

A Study in Scarlet also introduced Holmes's sidekick and foil, **Dr. Watson**, as well as master criminal **Professor Moriarty**. Watson is the detective's slow-witted and often bungling assistant who is always amazed at the brilliant crime-solving talents of his boss.

Doyle followed *A Study in Scarlet* with more Holmes tales—*The Sign of Four* (1890), and then a series of 24 short stories published in two separate volumes, *The Adventures of Sherlock Holmes* (1892) and *The Memoirs of Sherlock Holmes* (1894). The great success of these works enabled Doyle to abandon his medical practice and become a full-time writer.

However, Doyle had become tired of writing mystery fiction; in the last story of *The Memoirs of Sherlock Holmes*, he described Holmes's death at the hands of Professor Moriarty. The plot provoked such protests from readers that Doyle was forced to revive the popular character, beginning with *The Hounds of the Baskervilles* (1902). Eventually Doyle would write another 60 stories featuring the master sleuth.

With the publication of *A Study in Scarlet*, Doyle helped popularize the earliest form of the **detective story** genre of mystery fiction. His stories inspired stage productions and several movies. In addition, Sherlock Holmes tales developed followings through clubs, including the Baker Street Irregulars in New York—named for the detective's address at 221 Baker Street in London—and the Sherlock Holmes Society in London, groups which flourish to the present day.

Arthur Conan Doyle

57. The Jewish State
(1896) Theodor Herzl

Horrified by anti-Semitic sentiments in Europe, **Theodor Herzl** envisioned a place where the Jewish people could live freely without persecution. *The Jewish State*, Herzl's 1896 pamphlet later published as a book, called for the establishment of a state for Jews. His efforts led to the foundation of the **World Zionist Organization**, resulting in the eventual establishment of the state of **Israel**.

Herzl introduced his idea in an article in London's *Jewish Chronicle* in January 1896. Later that year, he published *Der Judenstaat (The Jewish State)*. In it, he argued that Jews could never be fully integrated into their adopted countries. They would always be considered outsiders.

"We are a people—one people. We have sincerely tried everywhere to merge with the national communities in which we live, seeking only to preserve the faith of our fathers. It

Theodor Herzl

is not permitted us. . . In our native lands where we have lived for centuries we are still decried as aliens, often by men whose ancestors had not yet come at a time when Jewish sighs had long been heard in the country. . ."

Herzl believed that it was not wise for Jews to assimilate in the countries in which they lived. Instead, he argued that the only way Jews could feel secure and find peace, was to have their own state—in the land which the Jews inhabited during Biblical times.

"**Palestine** is our unforgettable historic homeland. . . The Jews who will it shall achieve their State. We shall live at last as free men on our own soil, and in our own homes peacefully die. The world will be liberated by our freedom, enriched by our wealth, magnified by our greatness."

Herzl was born in 1860, in present-day Hungary. He received a law degree from the University of Vienna, but instead became a journalist and playwright.

After publication of *The Jewish State*, Herzl's ideas were met with enthusiasm by the Jewish masses in Eastern Europe, although some Jewish leaders believed his dream was impractical.

In 1897, Herzl invited Jewish representatives to the first **Zionist World Congress** in Basle, Switzerland. They agreed to seek establishment of a homeland for Jewish people. The Congress created the World Zionist Organization, naming Herzl president.

For years, Herzl met unsuccessfully with European leaders. Finally, the British government offered Uganda in East Africa as an interim homeland for Jews; however, the controversial proposal was rejected by the Zionist Congress of 1903. Herzl died the following year of pneumonia and heart problems.

In 1948, Herzl's dream was realized when the state of Israel was established in Palestine.

58. The War of the Worlds
(1898)   H.G. Wells

"No one would have believed in the last years of the nineteenth century that this world was being watched keenly and closely by intelligences greater than man's and yet as mortal as his own . . ." opens **H.G. Wells's** classic **science fiction** novel, *The War of the Worlds*.

Published in England in 1898, *The War of the Worlds* was the forerunner of an entire genre of science fiction stories that would become enormously popular in the 20th century.

The story is told by an unnamed narrator in and around the area of London. The book opens

Cover of 1963 edition of Wells's classic

with the storyteller describing how astronomers have seen a flame of gas shooting out from the planet **Mars**; a few days later, a cylinder lands in an area close to the narrator's home in a place called **Maybury Hill**.

Martians emerge from the cylinder; they are slow-moving, hideous-looking leathery creatures. They quickly fire a deadly heat ray into a crowd of nearby onlookers, killing them instantly. By good fortune, the narrator escapes.

Over the next several days, the invading Martians spread their terror, wiping out military troops sent to stop them. Using huge mechanical tripod machines, the invaders head for London, where news of the invasion has caused a panic, and residents try desperately to leave the city. After witnessing more battles in the countryside, and hiding from the Martians

for two days, the narrator travels to London. There he finds the entire Martian force dead or dying, killed by the bacteria on Earth, against which they had no immunity.

Wells created a dramatic and suspenseful story out of the most fantastic circumstances. There is a terrifying sense of dread throughout the story, and then, when the situation appears most hopeless, the story takes a surprising turn when the Martians, seemingly indestructible, succumb to the air in the Earth's atmosphere.

Born in Bromley, Kent, England in 1866, H.G. Wells gained fame in 1895 with publication of *The Time Machine*, followed two years later by *The Invisible Man*. He eventually produced more than 80 books spanning a 50-year writing career.

Forty years after its publication, *The War of the Worlds* received renewed notoriety when American actor and writer **Orson Welles** produced a radio adaptation of the story, transferred to New Jersey. The broadcast was so realistic it panicked thousands of listeners across the country, who believed a Martian invasion was actually taking place. The story, which has also been filmed, has served as a model for hundreds of science fiction tales about visitors from outer space.

59. The Interpretation of Dreams
(1900) Sigmund Freud

Dreams offer clues to our **unconscious minds**, **Sigmund Freud** revealed when he published *The Interpretation of Dreams* at the beginning of the 20th century.

Freud proposed a revolutionary theory by stating that dreams—even nightmares—represent repressed wishes, including sexual desires. He envisioned the mind as a battleground between conscious and unconscious thoughts, past and present, impulse and inhibition. Bringing the unconscious mind to light held the key to curing mental illness, Freud believed.

The language of dreams is disguised, often to conceal traumas from childhood, said Freud, who offered keys to unlock hidden meanings of dreams.

Freud wrote that objects or people appearing in dreams are often **symbolic**. A ghost, for example, may represent childhood memories of a mother in a pale nightgown visiting the child's room; wild animals may symbolize instinctive desires; mice or rats may symbolize annoying brothers or sisters.

Freud characterized the psyche as a battleground between the unconscious, or "**id**," and the conscious self, or "**ego**." Mental illness arose from repression of desires, he stated. A dream

Sigmund Freud

provides "the fulfillment of a [repressed] wish." Repressed wishes most often stem from childhood. According to Freud, "a wish which is represented in a dream must be an infantile one." Repression of wishes deemed inappropriate by the conscious mind—such as a wish to harm someone—may lead to anxiety and, in turn, to mental illness, Freud believed. He later established **psychoanalysis**, a method to resolve repressed traumas through a "talking cure."

Freud was born in 1856 in Freiburg, in present-day Czech Republic. His family moved to Vienna, Austria and Freud attended the university there as a medical student. He developed an interest in neurology, and later traveled to Paris and studied under French neurologist **Jean Charcot**, who used **hypnosis** to treat neurological conditions, such as hysterical paralysis.

Fascinated, Freud turned his attention to **psychotherapy**. Returning to Vienna, he opened a private practice specializing in nervous disease, but drew criticism from the medical profession for using Charcot's unorthodox methods.

Freud later abandoned hypnosis, and instead encouraged patients to use free association, or spontaneous flow of thoughts, to reveal the root of neurotic disturbance—and the subconscious meaning of dreams. He combined analysis of his patients' dreams and self-analysis of his own dreams. This research formed the basis for *The Interpretation of Dreams*, published in 1899, but dated 1900 to introduce Freud's ideas in the new century.

Though controversy over many of Freud's theories have continued for decades since his death in 1939, his discovery that unconscious thoughts and repressed childhood experiences could affect actions, emotions, and even physical well-being has gained widespread acceptance among medical professionals.

60. Up from Slavery
(1901)   Booker T. Washington

"I was born a slave . . . My life had its beginnings in the midst of the most miserable, desolate, and discouraging surroundings," African-American educator **Booker T. Washington** wrote in his inspirational autobiography, *Up from Slavery.*

Publication of *Up from Slavery*—which became both a national and international best seller—highlighted Washington's triumph over slavery and drew national attention to education issues for black Americans. "I have learned that success is to be measured not so much by the position that one has reached in his life," he wrote, "as by the obstacles which he has overcome while trying to succeed."

In *Up from Slavery,* Washington describes his rise from a poor uneducated slave to the head of an institution dedicated to helping blacks gain an education, learn a skill, and improve their status in society.

Born in West Virginia in 1856 to a black plantation cook and an unknown white father, Washington received no education, since it was illegal to teach slaves to read. After the Civil War ended, Washington packed salt and toiled in a coal mine, learning to read at night. At 16, determined to receive a formal education, he walked to the Hampton Normal and Agricultural Institute in Virginia, arriving penniless. He worked as a janitor while studying to become a teacher.

In 1881, he became head of the **Tuskegee Institute**, a newly established school for blacks. Undaunted by run-down buildings and meager funds, Washington transformed the school into one of the nation's leading higher education institutions over the next three decades.

Washington believed practical **vocational skills** would help former slaves become mainstreamed into society. Students at Tuskegee learned trades, such as carpentry, farming, and shoemaking. Pupils built school structures and even produced their own food.

Washington solicited donations from white industrialists, including Andrew Carnegie and John D. Rockefeller. He invited prominent educators to join the faculty, notably **George Washington Carver**, whose discoveries revolutionized southern agriculture.

Booker T. Washington

Washington favored a conciliatory, not confrontational approach to integrating blacks into society. He believed education was the key to improving economic conditions, enabling blacks to earn respect from whites and ultimately, legal equality.

However, during the early years of the 20th century, passage of segregation laws in the South and increasing violence against blacks led many to criticize Washington's views. His leadership role slowly declined, replaced by black leaders such as **W.E.B. DuBois**, cofounder of the **National Association for the Advancement of Colored People** (NAACP).

Yet, Washington's *Up from Slavery* served as an inspiration to many blacks during the 20th century. His emphasis on education as a key to black advancement has been embraced by civil rights advocates for more than 100 years.

61. The Story of My Life

(1902) Helen Keller

In *The Story of My Life*, **Helen Keller** describes her extraordinary transformation in an era when **disabled** individuals were often confined to institutions and considered uneducable.

Born in Alabama in 1880, Keller was the oldest child of a newspaper publisher. At the age of 19 months, she was stricken with an illness, possibly meningitis or scarlet fever, that left her blind, deaf, and mute.

Helen Keller

Abruptly deprived of sight and sound, Keller learned to rely on her other senses—touch, smell, and taste. By age 7, she had invented over 60 different signs to communicate. She touched people's lips, trying in vain to understand their words.

Frustrated by her limited ability to communicate, Keller began to throw tantrums—kicking, screaming, and hurling objects.

Her parents hired **Anne Sullivan** as a private tutor. Sullivan taught Keller the **manual alphabet**, pressing her fingers into the girl's hand to form letters. At first, Keller did not understand. However, when Sullivan led Keller to a pump, poured water over the child's hand and spelled out w-a-t-e-r, Keller became excited.

In *The Story of My Life*, Keller recalls the moment as the most important of her life:

"Suddenly I felt a misty consciousness as of something forgotten—a thrill of returning thought; and somehow the mystery of language was revealed to me. I knew then that 'w-a-t-e-r' meant the wonderful cool something that was flowing over my hand. That living word awakened my soul, gave it light, hope, joy, set it free!"

Keller also recalls the happiness she derived from sensing nature:

"Few know what joy it is to feel the roses pressing softly into the hand, or the beautiful motion of the lilies as they sway softly in the morning breeze. Sometimes I caught an insect in the flower I was plucking, and I felt the faint noise of a pair of wings rubbed together in a sudden terror . . ."

Later, Keller learned to read **Braille** and attended the Cambridge School for Young Ladies. In 1904, she graduated from **Radcliffe College**.

With help from Anne Sullivan and **John Macy**, a writer and publisher, Keller published *The Story of My Life* in 1903 as a three-part book. Part one was her autobiography. Part two featured her letters; part three was a description of her education written by Macy. The book's enormous success gave Keller and Sullivan financial independence.

Keller became a tireless crusader for the disabled and underprivileged. She wrote articles, lectured, and published 14 books. Before her death in 1968, Keller received many awards, including the Presidential Medal of Freedom.

62. The Call of the Wild
(1903)   Jack London

One of the most widely popular books with readers of all ages, *The Call of the Wild* is a classic tale of survival set in the **Alaskan wilderness**.

First published serially by the *Saturday Evening Post* in 1903, the story swiftly won popular and literary acclaim. Author **Jack London**—the pseudonym of **John Griffith Chaney**—chose the unusual literary technique of telling the story from the viewpoint of an animal, the sled dog, **Buck**.

The story traces Buck from his life as a pampered family pet through the ordeal that begins after an unscrupulous servant sells him to an unkind master, culminating in the dog's reversion to a wild animal. The dog's atavism—his throwback to a primitive nature—may be viewed as an allegory to the human condition.

"The snow walls pressed him on every side, and a great surge of fear swept through him— the fear of the wild thing for the trap."

Fear stirred ancestral memories, evoking a primitive response in Buck.

". . . instinctively, the hair on his neck and shoulders stood on end, and with a ferocious snarl he bounded straight up into the light of day."

The book was written shortly after London visited England; he was acutely aware of the contrast between conditions in English slums and the pristine beauty of the arctic region. Through Buck's viewpoint, London makes observations on life which apply equally to man and man's best friend. Buck's life-and-death struggle to survive in a hostile environment is symbolic of the struggle faced by working-class people in a capitalistic society.

Millions of readers have also enjoyed the purely entertaining nature of *The Call of the Wild*, which, like many of London's other works, was based on his own adventures.

Born in San Francisco in 1876, John Griffith Chaney assumed the nickname "Jack" and adopted his stepfather's surname. As a youth he worked at various odd jobs, and later traveled the country by rail as a hobo.

After briefly attending the University of California at Berkeley, in 1897, he left school to seek his fortune in the Klondike gold rush. He failed to find gold, but unearthed a wealth of material for his writings.

In 1900, publication of his first book, The *Son of the Wolf,* established his career as a writer. *The Call of the Wild* brought him international renown.

London made **realism** popular with the public, sounding a death knell for romantic idealism in literature. A lifelong socialist, London was the first author to gain widespread popularity among working class Americans, and his naturalistic style also influenced prominent literary successors, such as **Upton Sinclair** and **Ernest Hemingway**.

Jack London

63. The Jungle
(1906) Upton Sinclair

Upton Sinclair's disturbing novel, *The Jungle*, exposed dangerous and unsanitary conditions in the Chicago stockyards. The book sparked a federal investigation into meat-packing practices, leading to passage in 1906 of the **Pure Food and Drug Act** and the **Meat Inspection Act**.

As a result of *The Jungle*, Sinclair became the most famous of the "**muckrakers**," a term coined by President Theodore Roosevelt to refer to journalists who uncovered the hazards of industrialization. (The term derived from the "man with a muckrake" in John Bunyan's *The Pilgrim's Progress*.)

The Jungle centers around **Jurgis Rudkus**, a Lithuanian immigrant, whose dreams of finding wealth and freedom in America give way to disillusionment and despair. He discovers he has to pay graft to get his job, sweeping up guts for 17 cents an hour in a meatpacking factory where men sometimes fell into the boiling vats. Using graphic images, Sinclair

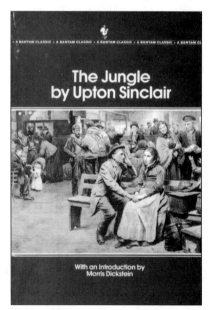

A 1981 edition of *The Jungle*

described Jurgis's first day working on the slaughterhouse floor:

". . . it was his place to follow down the line the man who drew out the smoking entrails from the carcass of the steer . . .it was a sweltering day in July, and the place ran with steaming hot blood—one waded in it on the floor. The stench was almost overpowering . . ."

Later Jurgis buys a house and is cheated by a contract he cannot read. He winds up in jail, but then finds salvation by joining the Socialist party. Sinclair wrote *The Jungle* to draw attention to the plight of the American working class—in this case, oppressed packinghouse workers suffering diseases, injuries, and death from unsafe conditions. Only a very small part of the novel actually describes the filth and chaos of meat processing in Packingtown—the fictional stand-in for Chicago. However, the descriptions were so vivid, and shocked so many Americans, that his work provoked a public outcry over impure foods. Sinclair later lamented, "I aimed at the public's heart, and by accident I hit it in the stomach."

Sinclair was born in 1878 in Baltimore, Maryland. When he was 19, he enrolled at Columbia University in New York. He also became active in the Socialist political movement, which influenced his writing throughout his life. He published several early novels, which sold poorly.

Sinclair went to Chicago to conduct research for *The Jungle*. Several publishers rejected the manuscript for its graphic descriptions and subject matter. In 1906, Sinclair succeeded in getting the novel published, and it evoked a public furor unrivaled since *Uncle Tom's Cabin* (see no. 45)

The Jungle stands as one of the most significant books ever published concerning social conditions in the United States.

In his classic, best-selling novel, *Riders of the Purple Sage*, **Zane Grey** popularized the **western** literary genre.

Grey extolled the natural beauty of the American West and the frontier values of its people. In his more than 80 books, he created memorable settings and characters idealizing the unwritten **Code of the West** embodying honor, loyalty, and self-reliance. More than 130 movies have been based on his books, including *Riders of the Purple Sage*, which has never been out of print since its initial publication.

The novel focuses on **Jane Withersteen**, a wealthy Mormon woman who inherits her father's ranch in the Utah desert, described in picturesque language:

"Her clear sight intensified the purple sage slope as it rolled before her. Low swells of prairie-like ground sloped up to the west. Dark, lonely cedar trees, few and far between, stood out strikingly, and at long distances ruins of red rock."

The story also features the character named **Lassiter**, who became a prototype for many western novels and films. A man with a mysterious past, he embodies the characteristics of both an outlaw and a hero. In the story, Jane Withersteen resists pressure from elders in the Mormon church to marry a polygamist with many wives. When the elders apply pressure by stampeding Withersteen's cattle, Lassiter rides to her rescue. As a showdown looms, he defends his use of violence:

"Where would any man be on this border without guns? . . . I'd be under the sage with thousands of other men . . ."

Ultimately, the troubled semi-outlaw Lassiter chooses the righteous path, saves the heroine, and finds love. It was a formula Grey would use time and again.

Grey's appreciation of frontier life stemmed from his heritage. Born **Pearl Grey** in 1872, he took his pen name from his birthplace, Zanesville, an Ohio town named for his ancestors. He grew up hearing family stories of pioneer homesteaders and other Western characters. In 1904, he published *Betty Zane*, a novel based on an ancestor's journal.

In 1907, Grey traveled to Arizona. On the trip, he became entranced with the West's rugged beauty and intriguing people, some of whom formed the basis for characters in *Riders of the Purple Sage*. He eventually moved west with his wife and children, acquiring a hunting lodge in Arizona and a house in California.

Riders of the Purple Sage was published in 1912, and sold two million copies. The story was filmed three times and became Grey's best-known western. After publishing a sequel, *The Rainbow Trail*, Grey went on to become the best-selling Western author of all time.

A 1940 edition of Grey's book

O Pioneers!
(1913) Willa Cather

Willa Cather's classic tale of life on the Nebraska prairie, *O Pioneers!*, is noted for its vivid descriptions of life among **Scandinavian immigrant pioneers**, and for its portrayal of a strong female main character.

Cather described **Alexandra Bergson** as "a tall, strong girl" who "walked rapidly and resolutely . . . She wore a man's long ulster (not as if it were an affliction, but as if it were very comfortable and belonged to her; carried it like a young soldier) and a round plush cap, tied down with a thick veil."

Willa Cather

After her father's death, Alexandra defies convention and runs a profitable farm—surviving droughts and blizzards—in an era when women were generally viewed as incapable of succeeding in business. She also raises her younger brother, but is devastated years later when he is murdered by a jealous husband. Ultimately, Alexandra finds solace and love, marrying her childhood sweetheart, **Carl Linstrum**.

Cather's writing brought to life the small town of Hanover, "anchored on a windy Nebraska tableland . . . trying not to be blown away. A mist of fine snowflakes was curling and eddying about the cluster of low drab buildings huddled on the gray prairie, under a gray sky."

Even the weather intensified the loneliness of both character and setting:

"The rattle of her wagon was lost in the howling of the wind, but her lantern, held firmly between her feet, made a moving point of light along the highway, going deeper and deeper into the dark country."

Cather's writing appealed to all of the senses. She describes Bohemians in a country store "drinking raw alcohol, tinctured with oil of cinnamon" to ward off the cold until "the overheated store sounded of their spirited language as it reeked of pipe smoke, damp woolens, and kerosene."

Alexandra's strong will and nonconformist actions closely resemble Cather's own lifestyle. Born in Virginia in 1873, she was nine when her family moved to Red Cloud, Nebraska, a small prairie town, where they lived among immigrant settlers.

Cather yearned to become a physician, and was also an aspiring actress. Both professions were frowned upon for respectable women, earning her the scorn of some townspeople.

She enrolled at the University of Nebraska, planning to study science, but later decided to pursue a career in journalism. In 1912, Cather turned to writing novels full-time, gaining almost immediate fame with the publication of *O Pioneers!* in 1913. In all she would write 12 novels, and earn a **Pulitzer Prize** in 1923.

O Pioneers! remains one of the defining portraits of immigrant life on the Great Plains during the late 19th century.

66. Sons and Lovers
(1913)   D.H. Lawrence

Sons and Lovers, **D.H. Lawrence's** working-class autobiographical novel set in an English mining town, uniquely combines vivid realism and elements of Freudian psychology.

The book probes the unconscious motivations of **Paul Morel**, son of a heavy-drinking coal miner and a domineering mother who becomes emotionally dependent on Paul after the death of Paul's brother. Paul's parents' marriage was a struggle, with constant friction arising from his mother's resentment of her husband's lower class status.

Paul develops an **Oedipus complex**, an unhealthy attachment to his mother that influences his future relationships. His early life experiences leave him unable to find romantic fulfillment as an adult with any woman who reminds him of the mother he has idealized. After her death he experiences grief, but also emotional release:

"Now she was gone, and for ever behind him was the gap in life, the tear in the veil, through which his life seemed to drift slowly . . ."

The novel also provides penetrating insights into the hardships faced by the working class during the **Industrial Revolution**. It exposed the impact of rapid industrialization and a materialistic society on individuals.

"The gin-pits were elbowed aside by the large mines of the financiers . . . the notorious Hell Row, which though growing old had acquired an evil reputation, was burned down, and much dirt was cleansed away," Lawrence wrote. What replaced Hell Row, however, was an environment that trapped miners in a cycle of poverty and deprivation.

Lawrence moved readers with emotional power, such as his description of William Morel's coffin being carried into the house:

". . .as the first men appeared, and the limbs and bowed heads of six men struggled to climb into the room, bearing the coffin that rode like sorrow on their living flesh. . ."

David Herbert Lawrence was born in Nottinghamshire, England, in 1885; he was the son of an illiterate coal miner and an educated mother who was a schoolteacher.

After graduating college, he became a teacher and then later turned to writing. Publication of *Sons and Lovers* in 1913 brought him literary fame.

Lawrence's life was plagued by severe health problems and personal turmoil. In addition, many of Lawrence's other works—including *Women in Love* (1921) and *Lady Chatterly's Lover* (1928)—generated controversy and censorship for their frank treatment of sexuality and unconscious desires.

Lawrence has gained esteem as a working-class novelist whose realistic style incorporated both natural instincts and psychological complexities. *Sons and Lovers* is considered by many to be his most outstanding novel.

D.H. Lawrence

67. Relativity: The Special and General Theory (1916) Albert Einstein

Albert Einstein

The world's most famous **physicist** joined the ranks of great teachers with publication of *Relativity: The Special and General Theory* in 1916.

Prior to its publication, even many scientists failed to fully understand **Albert Einstein's** complex theories. His book explained his principles of **relativity** in layman's terms, disclosing secrets of the universe to the general public.

Einstein's special theory of relativity stated that the speed of light was the same for all observers, regardless of their motion.

To explain his special principle of relativity, Einstein wrote, ". . . every motion must be considered only as a relative motion." A passenger in a railway carriage traveling at a uniform rate past an embankment which appears blurred might reach either of two justifiable conclusions: "The carriage is in motion relative to the embankment," or "The embankment is in motion relative to the carriage." If the carriage's motion is not uniform, "as for instance by a powerful application of the brakes, then the occupant . . . experiences a correspondingly powerful jerk forward," Einstein observed.

Einstein's special theory applies only to bodies moving in the absence of gravity. His general theory of relativity, by contrast, postulated that gravitational fields are equivalent to accelerations of the frame of reference. People in a moving elevator, for example, cannot tell whether the force acting on them is gravity or constant acceleration of the elevator. The general theory made the startling proposal that matter causes space to curve—and that time does not flow at a fixed rate.

Objects measurably change size and mass when traveling near the velocity of light, Einstein concluded. Mass could be converted into enormous quantities of energy, he revealed in his now-famous equation, **$E=mc^2$** (energy=mass x the speed of light squared).

Einstein was born in Germany in 1879. He demonstrated brilliance in math at an early age, but bored with school, he received poor grades and dropped out at the age of 15. Later, he studied physics and mathematics in Zurich, Switzerland.

In 1922, Einstein received the **Nobel Prize** in physics; in the 1930s, anti-Semitism in Germany led Einstein, a Jew, to settle in the United States, where he became a professor at Princeton University.

During World War, II Einstein wrote a letter warning President Roosevelt that Germany might be attempting to develop a bomb harnessing atomic energy. The letter spurred development of U.S. nuclear weapons, and the world witnessed shocking proof of his theory when the atomic bomb exploded over Hiroshima, Japan in 1945. As a pacifist, after the war Einstein became actively involved in the movement to abolish nuclear weapons.

68. Siddhartha

(1922) Hermann Hesse

The spiritual search for self-realization described in **Hermann Hesse's** lyrical novel *Siddhartha*, sparked interest in **Eastern religions** when it was first published in Europe in 1922. During the 1950s, it struck a chord among the Beat generation in America, where it developed a cult-like following among disenchanted youths.

Set in **India** during the time of **The Buddha** (c. 500 B.C.), the novel contains parallels to his life, but is not a fictionalized account of it. **Siddhartha**, son of a Brahmin, or Hindu priest, rejects his position of privilege. He takes up a life of asceticism, renouncing worldly pleasures in his quest for knowledge and salvation. He yearns "to become empty of thirst, desire, dreams, pleasure and sorrow . . . to experience the peace of an emptied heart, to experience pure thought."

Failing in his quest, he goes in search of **Gautama the Illustrious**, Buddha, a wandering holy man. Siddhartha rejects Buddha's doctrine of salvation, however, insisting he must find salvation on his own. He next immerses himself in sensual pleasures, but finds only emptiness. Despondent, he considers suicide.

At the River of Life, a ferryman shares the river's wisdom with Siddhartha. After learning that he has fathered a son, Siddhartha suffers bitter rejection when his son refuses to accept him. His pain fades, however, as he discovers his place in the universe. Listening closely to the water's flow, he hears the voices of the universe blend together. Ultimately, he finds his true 'Self':

"I learned through my body, and soul that it was necessary for me to sin . . . that I had to strive for property and experience nausea and the depths of despair in order to learn not to resist them, in order to learn to love the world . . .."

Siddhartha's search for truth spans both **Hindu** and **Buddhist** concepts of enlightenment, culminating in his discovery that while knowledge can be taught, wisdom must come from within.

Born in Germany in 1877, Hermann Hesse spent much of his life on his own spiritual quest. On a trip to India in 1911, Hesse became fascinated by Eastern mysticism and religions, which he later explored in *Siddhartha*.

Hermann Hesse

Beset by personal problems, Hesse underwent psychoanalysis for several years, and his later novels reflected his interest in psychology. In 1946, Hesse was awarded the **Nobel Prize** in literature.

After Hesse's death in 1962, a resurgence of interest in his writing occurred. By the mid-1970s, *Siddhartha* had gone through 22 reprintings. Interest waned in the 1980s, when criticism emerged of Hesse's Westernized views of Eastern religions. In the 1990s, however, the novel gained a new popularity among **New Age** readers seeking spiritual guidance.

69. Ulysses
(1922)   James Joyce

Ulysses, **James Joyce's** brilliant, controversial novel is considered by many critics to be the greatest literary work of the 20th century.

In this groundbreaking novel, Joyce experimented with new literary techniques, including "**stream of consciousness**," a method of portraying a character's flow of thoughts. To simulate the natural thought process, Joyce omitted punctuation, exhibited frank expressions, and made free use of fragmented ideas.

Ulysses details the lives of three ordinary people in Dublin, Ireland during a single day—June 16, 1904. The plot roughly parallels that of the *Odyssey,* the ancient Greek epic by **Homer**. The characters—**Stephen Dedalus**, **Leopold Bloom**, and his wife, **Molly**—correspond somewhat to the characters of Telemachus, Ulysses, and Penelope in the Homerian classic. However, Joyce uses a variety of literary and historic references to associate each character with many other figures as well.

Ulysses culminates in Molly Bloom's interior monologue of rambling reminiscences as she prepares for sleep, presented as an entire chapter composed solely in stream-of-consciousness style. In the following passage, she recalls an interlude in a flower garden:

". . . yes when I put the rose in my hair like the Andalusian girls used or shall I wear a red yes and how he kissed me under the Moorish wall and I thought well as well him as another and then he asked me would I yes . . ."

Ulysses' enormous length, its numerous themes—involving such subjects as mythology, European history, religion, and astronomy—and its mixture of a number of literary styles, have given the book the reputation of being one of the most complex novels written in the 20th century.

The book was first published in serial form in New York's *Little Review* in 1918. Serialization was suspended after the novel's frank sexual passages led to prosecution of the journal for publishing obscene material.

In 1922, a Paris bookstore owner published the complete novel. It remained banned in the United States until 1933, when in a landmark trial in New York, a judge ruled that the book was not obscene. It was then published by Random House.

James Joyce was born in Dublin in 1882 to a poor Catholic family. He attended Catholic schools and earned a degree in Latin from University College.

Suffering a crisis in faith, Joyce renounced Catholicism; dissatisfied by constraints of Irish life, he left Ireland permanently when he was 22. Joyce's autobiographical novel, *A Portrait of the Artist as a Young Man* (1916) established his reputation as a rising literary talent.

Publication of *Ulysses* brought Joyce international fame. It stands as a towering literary achievement by one of the 20th century's most noted authors.

James Joyce

70. The Great Gatsby

(1925)   F. Scott Fitzgerald

F. Scott Fitzgerald captured the spirit of the **Jazz Age** of the 1920s, and addressed the failure of the American dream in *The Great Gatsby*, a work that many critics consider the finest American novel of the 20th century.

The story is told by **Nick Carraway**, a mid-Westerner who moves to New York to become a stockbroker and get rich. There, a summer night party draws him into the glittering social whirl of his wealthy and flamboyant neighbor, **Jay Gatsby**:

"In his blue gardens men and girls came and went like moths among the whisperings and the champagne and the stars . . .The lights grow brighter as the earth lurches away from the sun, and now the orchestra is playing yellow cocktail music, and the opera of voices pitches a key higher. . ."

Gatsby's extravagance conceals inner conflicts, for he has reinvented his past in an effort to fit into a higher social class. Gatsby's naiveté is revealed when Nick warns that he can't repeat the past, to which Gatsy replies, "Why of course you can!"

Gatsby's renewal of an ill-fated romance with **Daisy Buchanan**, Nick's married cousin, leads to the collapse of Gatsby's dream, culminating in tragedy and his destruction. Ironically, Nick realizes at the funeral that, despite Gatsby's popularity when he was alive and hosting wild social affairs at his estate, Gatsby had almost no friends who truly cared about him.

Despite Gatsby's flaws, Nick admired his zest for life, which he terms "an extraordinary gift of hope." In the end, he reflects that although Gatsby's dream of recapturing the past seemed tantalizingly within reach, Gatsby failed to recognize that the dream "was already behind him." Gatsby's quest has been likened to the American dream; his failure symbolizes the defeat of idealism by greed in an era of social decadence.

F. Scott Fitzgerald

Francis Scott Fitzgerald was born in St. Paul, Minnesota, in 1896. He became instantly famous after the publication of his first novel, *This Side of Paradise* (1920), and he and his bride, **Zelda** got swept up in a celebrity lifestyle. They moved to France, drank heavily, and threw lavish parties. While there, Fitzgerald also wrote *The Great Gatsby*, which was published to widespread critical praise.

Zelda's health, and Fitzgerald's literary output, would suffer from their lifestyle. Financial trouble and then alcoholism ruined what was left of his career, and resulted in his death at age 44.

Despite Fitzgerald's tragic end, *The Great Gatsby* stands as a literary masterpiece, and the definitive novel about American life during the "**roaring twenties**."

71. Mein Kampf
(1925;1927) Adolf Hitler

In *Mein Kampf,* **Adolf Hitler** revealed his chilling plan to create a master **Aryan race** and to destroy those he viewed as inferior, particularly Jews.

Published in two volumes in 1925 and 1927, *Mein Kampf* (*My Struggle*) became the political manifesto of the **Nazi party**, appealing to German nationalism and militarism in the aftermath of Germany's bitter defeat in **World War I**.

Mein Kampf included Hitler's autobiographical account of his youth and rise within the Nazi party, as well as his beliefs on politics, race, and the future of Germany. Hitler considered the German people, or Aryans, to be a **"master race"** superior to all others. The Nazi party, he maintained, "feels itself obligated to promote the victory of the better and stronger, and demand the subordination of the inferior and weaker in accordance with the eternal will that dominates the universe."

Besides justifying the domination of "inferior" races, Hitler claimed that subjugated people "actually benefit by being conquered because they come in contact with and learn

from the superior Aryans." However, he maintained, to retain their superiority, Aryans should not intermarry with "inferior conquered people."

Hitler's strongest attack was reserved for those people of Jewish descent. "The mightiest counterpart to the Aryan is represented by the Jew," he stated. He then went on to describe a struggle for world domination as a racial, cultural, and political war pitting Aryans against Jews, whom he described as liars and parasites.

In the book, Hitler also justified military conquest of foreign lands. As the master race, he argued, Aryans were entitled to acquire more living space; conquered peoples would be eliminated or enslaved. Specifically, Hitler called for the defeat of Russia, which he believed was under control of Jewish Marxists, and the Slavic nations to the east, as well as France to the west.

The world's most destructive tyrant was born in 1889 in Austria. Hitler served in the German army in World War I, and after the war, he joined the National Socialist German Workers party, later called the Nazi party. In 1921, the party named Hitler its leader. Inflation and labor strikes fueled support for the Nazis.

In 1923, Hitler was jailed after a failed coup in Munich against the Bavarian government. In prison, he wrote the manuscript for *Mein Kampf.* He was released after only nine months, and his popularity—and the Nazi party's—continued to rise. In 1933, he became Germany's chancellor, assuming dictatorial powers.

By 1939, *Mein Kampf* had sold more than five million copies, but sadly, the world failed to take seriously the destructive intentions Hitler outlined in his book. The result was **World War II**, causing the deaths of more than 50 million people.

Hitler's picture from *Mein Kampf*

72. The Sun Also Rises
(1926) Ernest Hemingway

Inspired by a festival in **Pamplona, Spain**, where participants prove their courage by running with the bulls in the streets, journalist **Ernest Hemingway** wrote *The Sun Also Rises*. Told in terse, journalistic style, the book set the tone of the modern novel and vaulted Hemingway to international fame.

Focused on American and English expatriates in Europe, the story encompasses the anguish of the post-World War I "**Lost Generation.**" From the Left Bank of Paris to a bullfighting arena in Spain, characters search for meaning in their lives. The novel embodies Hemingway's code of principles—honor, courage, and dignity—qualities he found necessary in a world filled with moral ambiguities.

The central characters include **Lady Brett Ashley**, a flamboyant socialite, and her circle of admirers. The story's narrator is **Jake Barnes**, an American journalist scarred emotionally and physically by a war wound, who is unable to fulfill his love for Ashley.

Hemingway utilized short, repetitive phrases, as in Ashley's description of her attraction to a bullfighter:

"I can't help it. I've never been able to help anything . . . I can't stop things."

Hemingway captured a setting's essence in a minimum of words:

"The café was like a battleship stripped for action."

Brief dialogue conveyed ironic humor:

"I don't believe she would marry anybody she didn't love."

"Well," I said. "She's done it twice."

At the end of the story, nothing has really changed for any of the characters—and that is the point of the novel. For these people who are so "lost" and disillusioned, life has no direction, no meaning, and no future.

Hemingway's writing reflected his adventurous and highly publicized lifestyle. Born in a Chicago suburb in 1899 to a doctor and a

Ernest Hemingway

music teacher, he developed a love of adventure during summers spent at a Michigan lake.

As a reporter for the *Kansas City Star,* Hemingway learned to use short, declarative sentences. Rejected for military service due to an eye condition, he became an ambulance driver for the Red Cross during World War I. Wounded from machine gun fire and decorated for heroism, he fell in love with a nurse while hospitalized in Italy. He later used his war experiences in another of his best-known novels, *A Farewell to Arms* (1929).

Hemingway embodied rugged individualism. He hunted lions on safari, went deep-sea fishing, and enjoyed bullfighting. A war correspondent during World War II, he also aided the French Resistance and scouted Nazi submarines with his yacht.

Perhaps the most influential American author of modern times, Hemingway also suffered from a troubled private life. He committed suicide in Idaho in 1961.

73. The Oxford English Dictionary
(1928)

The *Oxford English Dictionary* is the most comprehensive authority on the history and evolution of the **English language** over the last one thousand years. A multi-volume work, it contains the **meaning**, **history**, and **pronunciation** of more than **500,000 words**.

Using an enormous array of international English language sources, from the Bible and classic literature, to film scripts and cookbooks, the *OED* traces the usage of words from all across the English-speaking world—North America to South Africa, Australia and New Zealand, and the Caribbean.

The dictionary had its origins in the 1850s, when it was first proposed by the **Philological Society** of London. At that time, the organization—dedicated to the study of the origin and meaning of words and literary texts—determined that existing English language dictionaries were inadequate. It called for a thorough re-examination of the language from around the year A.D. 1150. It was not until 1879, however, that the project got underway. That year the Society made an agreement with the **Oxford University Press** and a Scottish professor named **James A.H. Murray** to begin work on what was then called the *New English Dictionary*.

As principal editor, Murray put together a team and began to assemble the more than two tons of source quotations the Philological Society had collected. The project was originally scheduled to take about ten years to complete; however, after five years, Murray and his associates had only progressed as far as the word "ant." At that time, they knew they would have to seriously rethink their original timetable.

In 1884, the group did publish the dictionary's first part—or 'fascicle'—consisting of all their work up to that point. Over the next few decades, more than one hundred fascicles would be issued. Additional editors and their assembled staffs joined the project, and Murray continued to work on it until his death in 1915. Finally, in 1928 the complete 10-volume set, consisting of 15,490 pages containing 252,200 entries was published under the title, *A New English Dictionary on Historical Principles*.

In 1933, the dictionary was reissued in 12 volumes, together with a Supplement containing new words and meanings. The title was also officially changed to its current one—the *Oxford English Dictionary*. Over the next 50 years, additional Supplements were published, until in 1989, the *OED Second Edition* was published—a 20-volume set, consisting of 21,730 pages.

The various entries in the dictionary contain not only pronunciations and etymologies, but many are cross-referenced, illustrated, and cited in quotations from a wide variety of sources. The most frequently quoted work in the dictionary is the Bible, with approximately 25,000 quotations.

The 20-volume *Oxford English Dictionary* and its CD version

All Quiet on the Western Front has become the best-known novel set during **World War I**, depicting both the psychological and physical horrors of life in the battlefield trenches.

The author's chilling descriptions are based on his own experiences as a soldier during the war. Drafted into the **German army** in 1918, **Erich Maria Remarque** was wounded several times during his military service.

All Quiet on the Western Front is written in first-person viewpoint, told by **Paul Baumer**, a 19-year-old student urged by his schoolmaster to enlist in the German army. During the war, Paul forges strong friendships with his fellow soldiers.

The novel is among the first written in a style known as **social realism**, recounting everyday horrors in terse terms, as in this scene described by Paul:

"We see men living with their skulls blown open; we see soldiers run with their two feet cut off, they stagger on their splintered stumps into the next shell-hole . . . we find one man who has held the artery of his arm in his teeth for two hours in order not to bleed to death."

Confined in a foxhole bombarded by enemy shells, Paul is forced to stab a French soldier. The fallen soldier tumbles into the foxhole, where Paul comforts the Frenchman as he waits to die, empathizing with his youthful "enemy."

A 1958 edition of *All Quiet on the Western Front*

Later, Paul and a friend are wounded. Despite Paul's efforts to get medical help, his friend develops an infection and loses his leg through amputation.

Returning to the front, Paul suffers successive losses. One by one, his friends are killed. Ironically, one month before the end of the war, Paul suffers a fatal wound, accepting his fate with calm inevitability.

The book's author was born in Germany in 1898; he received his education at the University of Munster before serving in World War I. After the war, he worked as a race car driver and sportswriter while writing his novel.

Publication of *All Quiet on the Western Front* in 1929 touched a nerve among readers, sparking antiwar sentiments. In the 1930s, the book was banned by the Nazis, and later publicly burned. In 1938, Germany revoked Remarque's citizenship. He moved to Switzerland and later to the United States, where he became a naturalized citizen in 1947. After World War II, he moved back to Switzerland with his second wife, **Paulette Goddard**, an American actress.

Before his death in 1970, Remarque published several other novels. None, however, achieved the critical acclaim or had the impact of his first novel, *All Quiet on the Western Front*.

75. The Sound and the Fury
(1929) William Faulkner

The Sound and the Fury, **William Faulkner's** stirring tale of a decaying aristocratic southern family, is a groundbreaking novel in literary form and style, written by one of the 20th century's most influential authors.

Set in **Yoknapatawpha County**, a fictional rural region in Mississippi, the novel traces the decline of the once-wealthy **Compson family** after the Civil War. Following the tradition of **James Joyce**, Faulkner utilized stream-of-consciousness narration, and experimented further with shifting viewpoints and other nontraditional literary techniques.

The title of the novel derives from Shakespeare's **Macbeth**, which refers to a tale "told by an idiot, full of sound and fury." Faulkner divided the story into **four sections**, and each section is presented by a different narrator. Three of the

William Faulkner

sections are interior monologues of the three Compson brothers. The final section is a third-person narrative that focuses on a black servant and cook.

The novel opens from the viewpoint of a mentally retarded man, **Benjy**, youngest of the Compson sons. His disjointed narrative includes surprising flashes of perception, revealing a disturbing dark side to the family history.

Benjy recalls seeing his sister, **Caddy**, in a creek:

"Caddy was all wet and muddy behind, and I started to cry and she came and squatted in the water."

As Caddy climbed a tree, Benjy and his brothers observed from below:

"We watched the muddy bottom of her drawers. Then we couldn't see her. We could hear the tree thrashing."

Caddy's soiled garments foreshadowed the sullying of her purity; vanishing into the tree symbolized her later disappearance from her brothers' lives.

The second section is told by **Quentin**, a neurotic college student whose world revolves around family honor and his sister, Caddy; and the third section is narrated by the greedy and heartless Jason. The final section focuses on **Dilsey**, the faithful black cook, whose compassion and patience contrasts sharply with the self-absorption and self-destructiveness of the Compsons.

Born William Falkner in New Albany, Mississippi in 1897, the author was descended from an old southern family. A broken romance spurred him to join the British Royal Air Force in World War I. To pass as British, he added a "u" to his surname, reinvented his birthplace, and feigned an English accent. His pilot training ended with the 1918 Armistice.

After briefly attending college, Faulkner moved to New Orleans, and became a journalist. In 1926, his first novel, *Soldier's Pay*, was published, and three years later, *The Sound and the Fury*.

The author of many other notable books, including *Light in August* (1932) and *Absalom, Absalom!* (1936), Faulkner was awarded the **Nobel Prize** in literature in 1949. Many critics consider *The Sound and the Fury* his finest work.

Dashiell Hammett virtually invented the hard-boiled **detective genre** of fiction when he wrote *The Maltese Falcon* in 1930.

Until Hammett's novel, fictional detectives had been modeled on inquisitive, mannered, and deliberative characters such as Sir **Arthur Conan Doyle's** British detective, **Sherlock Holmes**.

With *The Maltese Falcon*, Hammett created an entirely different—and distinctly American—type of detective: **Sam Spade**, a sharp-witted private eye who "looked rather pleasantly like a blond Satan." While Spade never intentionally tries to break the law, he's not above stretching its limits and manipulating everyone involved in his case, including the police, the criminals, and even his own clients, to accomplish his goal—the search for the truth.

The story is filled with numerous twists and turns. As the plot unfolds, two men are murdered, and Spade is the chief suspect in their deaths. He becomes determined to find the real killer and clear his name. However, the story soon shifts focus, as Spade and a host of wildly colorful, nefarious characters become obsessed with the search for a 400 year-old priceless jewel-encrusted statue of a falcon.

Hammett wrote in a terse, ironic style, similar to novelist **Ernest Hemingway**. Hammett's dialog crackles with a "hard-boiled" cynicism, as when he reveals Spade's attitude towards authority:

"At one time or another I've had to tell everyone from the Supreme Court down to go to hell, and I've got away with it."

At the end, Spade outmaneuvers the criminals, the police, and his even own client, who tries to buy his silence to conceal her own complicity. When she refuses to believe he's going to turn her in to the police, he says:

"Don't be too sure I'm as crooked as I'm supposed to be."

His explanation for his behavior is simple:

"When a man's partner is killed, he's supposed to do something about it."

The author created a memorable story out of his own personal background. Samuel Dashiell Hammett was born in 1894 in Maryland; at the age of 21, he joined the **Pinkerton National Detective Agency**. He worked as an operative for six years, traveling across the country on assignments.

After Hammett quit Pinkerton, he began to publish fiction stories for pulp magazines under the pseudonym **Peter Collinson**. Later, he assumed the pen name Dashiell Hammett.

Hammett's literary output consisted of four other novels, and numerous short stories. All were written in the same hard-boiled style as *The Maltese Falcon*. The book inspired three movies, including the 1941 classic starring **Humphrey Bogart**.

The genre Hammett created influenced hundreds of other detective novelists, including such notables as **Raymond Chandler** and **Ross MacDonald**, and permanently infused gritty realism into American crime fiction.

A 1972 edition of
The Maltese Falcon

One of the 20th century's most popular novels, **Pearl Buck's** *The Good Earth*, played a major role in shaping Western attitudes towards **China**.

The novel relates conflicts faced by **Wang Lung**, an impoverished peasant farmer who rises to prosperity as a landlord, and his devoted wife, **O-lan**. The book opens with a description of Wang Lung's wedding day. Buck's Biblical-style prose emphasizes the importance of the earth itself as a source of life:

"The fields needed rain for fruition. There would be no rain this day, but within a few days, if this wind continued, there would be water. It was good. . . Now it was as if Heaven had chosen this day to wish him well. Earth would bear fruit."

Wang Lung's bride, O-lan, has been a slave since childhood in the **House of Hwang**. Bride and groom are strangers before their marriage. A traditional woman, O-lan takes

Pearl Buck

pride in her role as wife and mother despite the hard work.

The novel provides insights into the lives of rich landowners and poor peasants, tracing the rise of the Wang family and the fall of the wealthy Hwang family. Selling off the family's land leads to destruction, a lesson Wang Lung learns too late. Ultimately, the book reveals that when land is lost "it is the end of a family."

A New York Times critique by Kiang Kang-Hu, a professor at McGill University in Montreal, contended that Buck inaccurately portrayed Chinese life. In a rebuttal, Buck defended her work, adding that Kiang "wants China to be represented to the eyes of the Western world by its scholars and intellectuals—not by its peasants and common people."

Pearl Buck knew about Chinese life from first-hand experience. She was born **Pearl Comfort Sydenstricker** in West Virginia in 1892; her parents were American missionaries who moved to China when she was an infant. She grew up amid peasants in a rural community and remained in China for most of the next 40 years.

After graduating from college in the United States, she returned to China where she married agricultural economist John Lossing Buck. She began publishing stories and essays about China in American magazines, and in 1930, published her first novel, *East Wind, West Wind.*

In 1931, *The Good Earth* vaulted onto best-seller lists, opening Americans' eyes to life in China during the last emperor's reign. The novel, which was eventually translated into 30 languages, won a **Pulitzer Prize** for fiction in 1932, and inspired a Broadway play and a motion picture.

In 1938, Pearl S. Buck became the first American woman to be awarded a **Nobel Prize** in literature.

78. Brave New World
(1932) Aldous Huxley

Aldous Huxley's futuristic, satiric novel, *Brave New World*, sounded an early warning about potential dangers of runaway technology and its negative effects on society.

Decades before genetic engineering became a scientific reality, Huxley's 1932 novel envisioned a **dystopian**—anti-utopian—**society** in which humans are reproduced in laboratories, genetically engineered to accept predestined roles. Mind-altering drugs, prohibitions against religion, and manipulative media allow the government to further control individuals in *Brave New World*.

In Huxley's story, human embryos are developed in bottles and conditioned to collectivism and passivity. Those who fail to conform to societal standards become outcasts, exiled to the **Savage Reservation**, where hedonistic pleasures prevail.

When a "savage" is found and brought into the society of the "Brave New World" as an experiment, he rebels against authoritarian domination. As a self-educated individual—the savage obtained his education from reading Shakespeare—he believes in spirituality and moral choice.

"But I don't want comfort. I want God. I want poetry. I want real danger. I want freedom. I want goodness. I want sin."

"In fact," said Mustapha Mond, "you're claiming the right to be unhappy."

"All right then, said the Savage defiantly. "I'm claiming the right to be unhappy."

Huxley's interest in the moral implications of science had roots in his ancestry. Born in Surrey, England in 1894, he was the grandson of **Thomas Henry Huxley**, a famous biologist who helped develop the theory of evolution.

While in school at Eton, Huxley was stricken with keratitis, which left him nearly blind. He later recovered partial vision, enabling him to attend Oxford University. While his poor vision prevented him from becoming a doctor

or scientist, after regaining sufficient eyesight to read with a magnifying glass, he pursued a literary career. In 1921, he published his first novel, *Crome Yellow*.

In the early 1930s, when Huxley was writing *Brave New World*, advances in science were heralded as progress. Huxley's novel alerted the public to potential perils—presenting a world in which man became subservient to technology. Huxley objected to the notion that heredity bred superiority, another theme he explored in *Brave New World*.

Aldous Huxley

Huxley developed an interest in Hindu philosophy and transcendental mysticism, themes he later explored in such works as, *Eyeless in Gaza* (1936). In 1958, Huxley wrote *Brave New World Revisited*, which addressed problems ranging from overpopulation to psychological brainwashing.

When *Brave New World* was first published, few people believed that the scenario he described could become technologically feasible. By the dawn of the 21st century, scientific possibilities foreseen by Huxley became reality, causing the literary community to acknowledge the startling accuracy of Huxley's prophetic vision.

Story of Civilization
(1935-1975) Will and Ariel Durant

Will Durant

Ariel Durant

One of the most ambitious literary projects ever undertaken, the *Story of Civilization* is an **11-volume** narrative spanning 15,000 years of **human history**.

A collaborative effort by the husband and wife team of **Will** and **Ariel Durant**, *Story of Civilization* traces the development of mankind from ancient times through the reign of the French Emperor Napoleon in the early 19th century.

The set, published from 1935 to 1975, consists of *Our Oriental Heritage, The Life of Greece, Caesar and Christ, The Age of Faith, The Renaissance, The Reformation, The Age of Reason Begins, The Age of Louis XIV, The Age of Voltaire, Rousseau and Revolution,* and *The Age of Napoleon.* Some of the volumes are more than 1,000 pages in length.

Unlike many academic texts, *Story of Civilization* is not a dry recitation of names and dates. Instead, the Durants used an entertaining style of storytelling, adding colorful details to bring history to life.

The authors captured the essence of historical figures, often in pithy phrases. For example, in *The Reformation* they write that "Charles V was the most impressive failure of his age, and even his virtues were sometimes unfortunate for mankind."

The Durants' belief in the interconnectedness of history, its major figures, and their ideas is evident in their very first volume of their massive study. In *Our Oriental Heritage* Durant writes,

"Life oscillates between Voltaire and Rousseau, Confucius and Lao-Tze, Socrates and Christ. After every idea has had its day with us and we have fought it not wisely or too well, we in our turn shall tire of the battle, and pass on to the young our thinning fascicle of ideals."

Born in Massachusetts in 1885, Will Durant graduated from Columbia University. While teaching at the Ferrer Modern School in New York, he fell in love with a young student named Ada Kaufman, whom he nicknamed Ariel. In 1913, they married and the bride later changed her name to Ariel Durant.

The couple spent four decades collaborating on *Story of Civilization*, working 8 to 14 hours daily. They traveled the globe several times conducting their research. Although Ariel contributed to each volume, her efforts were not acknowledged initially. As her workload grew, her name was added as a co-author on the last five volumes.

In 1967, the Durants won a **Pulitzer Prize** for their tenth volume, *Rousseau and Revolution.* In 1976, President Gerald Ford awarded a **Presidential Medal of Freedom** to the couple for their contributions, which he observed "have made the past more vivid and enriched our lives in the present

Both Will and Ariel Durant died in 1981.

80. Gone with the Wind
(1936) Margaret Mitchell

Gone with the Wind, **Margaret Mitchell's** epic saga of the South, is among the most widely-read novels ever written.

Since its first publication in 1936, the book has sold nearly 30 million copies in over 37 countries. In 1937, it won a **Pulitzer Prize**.

An epic love story set during the **Civil War** and the aftermath of Reconstruction, the book's heroine is **Scarlett O'Hara**, a strong-willed, defiant, and manipulative Southern belle. Scarlett's love for the dashing and gentle **Ashley Wilkes** is unrequited, as he marries the gentle and loving **Melanie Hamilton**. Twice widowed, Scarlett then marries the fiery **Rhett Butler**, who is more than a match for her willful ways. Told from a sympathetic Southern point of view, the novel, portrays characters struggling to survive as the Old South crumbles:

Margaret Mitchell

> "There was a land of Cavaliers and Cotton Fields
> Called the Old South. Here in this Pretty World
> Gallantry took its last bow . . . Look for it only in books,
> For it is no more than a dream remembered.
> A civilization gone with the wind . . ."

"I wrote about the people who had gumption and the people who didn't," Mitchell said.

Born in 1900 in Atlanta, Georgia, Mitchell grew up listening to stories of ancestors who fought in the Civil War. During the 1920s, she became a newspaper reporter, and after arthritis forced her to quit her job, her husband gave her a typewriter and suggested she write a book.

Mitchell spent years writing her masterpiece. After its publication, she heard from fans worldwide—all anxious to know if Scarlett would reunite with Rhett.

The book was such an enormous and instant success, that speculation over who would star in the Hollywood film version made national news headlines. Reportedly, producer David O. Selznick who bought the film rights, paid the huge sum of $50,000 to Mitchell before he'd even read the book. With virtual unknown British actress **Vivien Leigh** and well-known Hollywood star **Clark Gable** in the lead roles, the film version was made in 1939; it became one of the most popular movies of all time, winning 11 Academy Awards.

While Mitchell supposedly planned to write a sequel, tragically she never wrote another book. In 1949, she was struck by a car and killed.

Four decades later, Mitchell's estate authorized author **Alexandra Ripley** to write a sequel to *Gone with the Wind*. Fans eager to learn the fates of Rhett and Scarlett rushed to buy copies, but the book received poor reviews.

No other book, critics concurred, could match Margaret Mitchell's unforgettable saga of the vanquished South.

81. The Grapes of Wrath
(1939) John Steinbeck

One of the most effective stories of social protest in American history, **John Steinbeck's** *The Grapes of Wrath* exposed disillusionment, injustices, and abuses suffered by **migrant workers** during the **Great Depression**. Published in 1939, the poignant novel won critical acclaim and spurred enactment of government agricultural reforms.

John Steinbeck

During the 1930s, droughts and dust storms in the American Great Plains caused topsoil to blow away, leaving millions of acres of farmland barren. Thousands of families lost their farms, and many of them headed west looking for work and a new place to live.

The Grapes of Wrath describes the hardships of one such family, the impoverished **Joads**, who leave Oklahoma's dust-bowl region for California in search of work as migrant fruit-pickers. However, with so many people look-ing for work during the Great Depression, they find that when they reach California they're not welcome. Scorned as "Okies," they're taken advantage of by the wealthy agri-cultural growers, and mistreated by the local police, who fear that large numbers of dissatis-fied workers might cause labor unrest.

"There is sorrow here that weeping cannot symbolize," Steinbeck wrote, as he described fruit doused with kerosene and allowed to rot while workers and their families starved. ". . . in the eyes of the hungry there is a grow-ing wrath. In the souls of the people the grapes of wrath are filling and growing heavy, growing heavy for the vintage."

While the Joads endure the deaths of fami-ly members, son Tom's implication in a mur-der and his flight, and efforts by the growers to break workers' spirits, the family retains its dignity. At the end of the novel, the family is defeated, but determined to survive.

"They ain't gonna wipe us out," Ma Joad insists. "Why, we're the people—we go on."

Born in Salinas, California in 1902, Steinbeck attended Stanford University intermittently before leaving for good after he published some poems and short stories. Traveling to New York, he worked as a reporter before returning to California, where he labored as a ranch hand and fruitpicker.

In California, Steinbeck witnessed first-hand the plight and shameful treatment of migrant families. Disturbed by what he saw, he wrote *The Grapes of Wrath*. It won a **National Book Award** and a **Pulitzer Prize**, and inspired an award-winning motion pic-ture in 1940.

Steinbeck published other widely-praised novels, including *Of Mice and Men* (1937), *Cannery Row* (1945), *East of Eden* (1952), and *The Winter of Our Discontent* (1961). In 1962, he received the **Nobel Prize** in literature.

John Steinbeck died in 1968.

82. Native Son

(1940) Richard Wright

Native Son, **Richard Wright's** novel of an African-American man trapped in a downward spiral of poverty, injustice, and violence, changed perceptions of **the black experience** in America.

The novel dispelled the myth of the patient, subservient black man previously conveyed in many books and films. Instead, *Native Son* forced readers to confront the poverty and oppression experienced by inner-city black Americans, conditions that created feelings of hopelessness and rage.

The novel centers around **Bigger Thomas,** a young black man living in **Chicago's slums** during the 1930s. From its opening scene, in which Bigger confronts a rat with a frying pan in his family's apartment, readers are drawn to the environment shaping Bigger's future.

After taking a job as a chauffeur for a prominent white family, Bigger becomes caught up in a cycle of fear and violence, culminating in his rejection of white oppression and his rationalization of murder:

"When a man kills, it's for something . . . I didn't know I was really alive in this world until I felt things hard enough to kill for 'em."

Bigger commits two murders, is defended in court by a Communist attorney, and is condemned to death. Ironically, by creating a character so scarred by racism that the reader loses sympathy for the individual, Wright focuses attention on the societal conditions that created a climate of inhumanity. *Native Son* was based partly on the true case of a young Chicago black man convicted of murder and executed in 1938, and partly on the author's own background.

Born on a plantation in Natchez, Mississippi in 1908, Richard Wright grew up impoverished in the segregated South. In 1924, a southern black newspaper printed his first short story. He held odd jobs through-out the South before moving to Chicago in 1927. In 1936, he became an activist in the Communist party and wrote articles for labor publications. In 1938, *Uncle Tom's Children,* a collection of his stories, was published.

Native Son brought him wide literary recognition. The book became a play and later a motion picture, with Wright himself playing the lead role. In 1944, Wright severed his ties to Communism and the next year he published *Black Boy,* an autobiographical novel based on his childhood. Discouraged by continuing racism in America, Wright moved to Paris, where he lived until his death in 1960.

Native Son was a hard, sobering look at America's treatment of blacks, and its publication helped galvanize activists, who began a concerted effort to improve conditions for black Americans, culminating in the passage of civil rights laws 25 years later.

Richard Wright

Dr. **Benjamin Spock's** book, The *Common Sense Book of Baby and Child Care*, revolutionized concepts of **parenting** for an entire baby-boom generation born after World War II.

When it was first published, Spock's book was the only manual on **child care** which did not advocate a more traditional "hardline" approach to child rearing. For centuries, parents had been discouraged from showing affection to children and were encouraged to enforce rigid schedules for their youngsters' feedings, toilet training, and sleep. Spock defied tradition by advising parents to openly demonstrate affection, allow flexibility in scheduling, listen to children's concerns, and trust their own good judgment. He also doled out practical advice on matters ranging from diaper rash to colic.

The Common Sense Book Baby and Child Care was made widely available as an inexpensive paperback, and it was an immediate enormous success. It sold three million copies during its first three years; by the time of Spock's death in 1998, more than 50 million copies had been sold in 42 languages.

Born in 1903 in New Haven, Connecticut, Benjamin Spock had a comfortable childhood. His father, an attorney, deferred child-rearing duties to Spock's mother, who lavished affection on her son while also instilling discipline.

Spock attended Yale University, and after graduating from the College of Physicians and Surgeons at Columbia University in New York, he opened a pediatric practice.

The young doctor realized that many patients' problems were behavioral, not medical. Parents complained that children threw tantrums and refused to eat or toilet-train according to rigid schedules. Spock was also appalled by advice given out by some doctors, such as putting iodine on infants' hands to halt thumb-sucking.

Believing in a better approach to parenting, he wrote *The Common Sense Book of Baby and Child Care*. In addition to its quick popularity, it also started a new trend in publishing: numerous "popular" medical books by qualified authors that tried to explain things to the average reader in a simple and understandable manner.

During the Vietnam War, Spock devoted himself to the antiwar movement, concerned that a generation of "Spock babies" were dying in combat. In 1968, he was convicted of conspiring to aid resistance to the draft. He spent two years in prison before his conviction was overturned.

During the social unrest of the 1960s, critics tried to discredit him, claiming his "permissive" child-rearing tactics had caused societal ills, although Spock's book always stressed the importance of setting limits on children's behavior.

Spock authored several other books on raising children, and until his death at age 94, he drafted updates to his child care manual, including a final revision published posthumously.

Benjamin Spock

84. Anne Frank: The Diary of a Young Girl (1947) Anne Frank

"In spite of everything, I still believe that people are really good at heart," **Anne Frank**, a young **Jewish** girl, wrote in her diary while in hiding from the **Nazis** during **World War II**. Published after her death, *Anne Frank: The Diary of a Young Girl* reveals her indomitable spirit that triumphed above the degradations she and her family were forced to endure.

Born in Germany in 1929, Anne moved with her family to **Amsterdam**, **Holland** in 1933 to escape increasing persecution of Jews. After Holland fell to invading German forces in 1940, Anne was forced to transfer to a school for Jewish children.

On her 13th birthday, she received a diary as a gift from her parents. A few weeks after Anne began confiding her innermost thoughts, her sister, Margot, received a notice to report to a concentration camp.

Anne's family went into hiding in a secret annex above her father's food import business on July 9, 1942. They were joined by the **Van Pelz** family (called "Van Daan" in Anne's diary), including the couple's 15 year-old son, Peter. Later, a dentist, **Albert Dussel**, shared the families' hiding place.

For two years, they survived on food and supplies smuggled in by non-Jewish friends, who also brought disturbing news.

"Our many Jewish friends . . . are being taken away in droves," Anne wrote upon hearing of "cattle cars" transporting Jews to a concentration camp. "We assume that most of them are being murdered. The English radio says they're being gassed."

Despite the horrors of war, Anne also recounted joys during her confinement, describing her flowering womanhood and budding romantic feelings for Peter Van Pelz.

In 1944, Dutch informers betrayed the families' hiding place. In August, the Frank family was sent to the **Auschwitz concentration camp** in Poland, where Anne's mother

Anne Frank

died. Anne and her sister were transferred to **Bergen-Belsen**, a concentration camp in Germany, where both died of typhoid fever in April, 1945.

Of the eight people confined to the secret annex, only Anne's father, Otto, survived. After the war ended, he received Anne's diary from friends, who had found it in the annex. Deeply moved by her words, he had the diary published in 1947, originally under the title *Het Achterhuis (The Diary of a Young Girl)*.

Translated into 55 languages, it has become one of the world's most widely read books. A new English translation published in 1995 includes material previously omitted. The diary also inspired a Pulitzer Prize-winning play and a motion picture.

The diary has been profoundly effective at conveying the horror of the **Holocaust**—both in the enormity of its tragedy, and in the personal humanity of its individual victims.

85. Cry, the Beloved Country
(1948) Alan Paton

A 1950 edition of *Cry, the Beloved Country*

Alan Paton's *Cry, the Beloved Country*, published to international acclaim in 1948, drew the world's attention to **racial intolerance in South Africa**.

Set in a South African village during the turbulent 1940s, the novel weaves a poignant tale of two fathers—a black man, **Stephen Kumalo**, a Zulu tribal minister, and a white man, **James Jarvis**. Oppression of blacks by the nation's white minority culminates in Kumalo's only son, Absalom, killing Jarvis's only son. Linked by tragedy, the two fathers must learn to work together.

The novel's message is revealed through **Msimangu**, a Zulu, who observes, "I see only one hope for our country, and that is when white men and black men, desiring neither power or money, but desiring only the good of their country, come together to work for it."

Written in a lyrical language at times, the novel foreshadows violent truths underlying the beauty. The story begins with a description of "a lovely road that runs from Ixopo into the hills," but then Paton describes the land after a storm where "the dead streams come to life, full of the red blood of the earth."

When *Cry, the Beloved Country* was written, South Africa was bitterly divided by segregation and prejudice. Political power was controlled by the white minority population, and the blacks suffered poverty and a dissolution of native tribal culture.

Three months after *Cry, the Beloved Country* was published, the white **National party** won election and soon formally instituted policies of racial **apartheid**, or "separateness." Apartheid laws mandated separate living areas, schools, and employment opportunities for whites and blacks.

Cry, the Beloved Country focused global attention on South Africa's rigid apartheid laws. The fact that the story was written by a white South African native added to the novel's notoriety.

Born in South Africa in 1903, Alan Paton graduated from the University of Natal, and went on to teach at a native school in the village of Ixopo. Although he was a white man, he grew disturbed by degradation of the nation's black majority.

Publication of *Cry, the Beloved Country* brought Paton international recognition. He used his celebrity status to seek justice for black South Africans. In 1953, he became the first president of the nation's **Liberal party**, advocating alternatives to apartheid.

In 1968, the government forced the Party to dissolve. Paton's passport was seized to stop him from traveling abroad and criticizing government policies. Paton continued his opposition to apartheid, garnering many awards for his humanitarian efforts.

Two years after Paton's death in 1988, South Africa's white government began to dismantle the system of apartheid; in 1994, the black majority came to power with the election of **Nelson Mandela** as president.

86. The Second World War
(1948-1954) Winston Churchill

The Second World War, **Winston Churchill's six-volume** history of **World War II**, is one of the most remarkable first-hand accounts of a significant period in world history since Julius Caesar wrote about the Gallic Wars two thousand years earlier.

Published over a six-year period, the volumes are: *The Gathering Storm, Their Finest Hour, The Grand Alliance, The Hinge of Fate, Closing the Ring,* and *Triumph and Tragedy.*

In *The Gathering Storm,* Churchill describes the shaky peace that ended World War I, the rise of Adolf Hitler's Nazi party, and Germany's increasing encroachment of European lands beyond its borders. Throughout the late 1930s, Churchill had been quite vocal about the increasing German threat, warnings that went unheeded by all of Europe's leaders. *The Gathering Storm* ends with Churchill's vindication, as he becomes England's leader in May, 1940, when the **German war machine** was already wreaking havoc on the continent. Churchill recalls that, "I felt as if I were walking with destiny, and that all my past life had been a preparation for this hour and for this trial."

In volume two, *Their Finest Hour,* Churchill describes **England's isolation** in the fight against Germany in 1940 after the fall of France. The courage of the British people, and Churchill's own experiences during the **Blitz**, make this a memorable narrative.

Winston Churchill

Volumes three, four and five, take the war from 1941 to the eve of D-Day. Germany's attack on the Soviet Union opening up the war on the Eastern Front, the Japanese attack on Pearl Harbor, bringing the United States into the conflict, the long campaigns in Africa and Italy, and Churchill's meetings with **Franklin D. Roosevelt** and **Josef Stalin** are all described. Churchill closes the fifth volume with the allies poised to reclaim the European continent: "All the ships were at sea. We had the mastery of the oceans and of the air. The Hitler tyranny was doomed."

The final volume carries the war to its conclusion, and its aftermath. Churchill reveals his reaction to the death of President Roosevelt—"I felt as if I had been struck a physical blow"— shortly before the allies complete the conquest of Nazi Germany.

Ironically, Churchill himself would not be in power for the war's ultimate end— the surrender of Japan. In the July, 1945 general elections, Britain voted in a Labor party government, and the Conservative Churchill resigned immediately.

Churchill spent his post-war career writing other books, and regaining political power during the 1950s, when he once again served as prime minister (1951-1955). He won the **Nobel Prize** in literature in 1953. When he died in 1965, British Prime Minister Clement Atlee eulogized Churchill as "the greatest citizen of the world of our time."

87. The Catcher in the Rye
(1951) J.D. Salinger

Teenage rebellion and the cynicism of adolescence came to life as never before in **J.D. Salinger's** *The Catcher in the Rye*, one of the most influential young adult novels to come out of the post-World War II era.

Following in the tradition of **Mark Twain**, Salinger used wry insights and colorful language to present young **Holden Caulfield's** experiences on the streets of **New York**, and his subsequent mental and physical breakdown.

The narrator, 16-year-old Holden, introduces himself this way:

"If you really want to hear about it, the first thing you'll probably want to know is where I was born and what my lousy childhood was like . . . and all that David Copperfield kind of crap, but I don't feel like going into it . . ."

Cover of 2001 paperback edition

Not eager to face his parents after his expulsion from prep school, Holden heads for New York City. There, he spends several days on the streets, where he encounters a variety of characters including taxi drivers, nuns, a prostitute, and a former teacher. Through Holden's eyes, Salinger reveals a disjointed world in which the teenager's delinquencies seem trivial compared to the less-than-scrupulous actions of adults.

Holden's efforts to escape from a nightmare reality through alcohol and meaningless encounters prove futile. It becomes evident that the teen needs affection and positive attention, which his parents have failed to provide. Ultimately, he is saved by his sister, the one person who truly cares for Holden; the end of the novel finds him recovering in a sanitarium.

Salinger used repetition, humor, and colorful slang to infuse reality into his teenage protagonist's speech, while revealing Holden's moodiness and emotional detachment.

Holden's feelings of **alienation** and efforts to make sense of the adult world struck a responsive chord among the post-World War II generation of high school and college students. The novel developed a popular following, while also winning critical acclaim.

Author Jerome David Salinger grew up in New York City, where he was born in 1919. He attended public schools and a military academy. After taking a writing class at Columbia University, Salinger began writing short stories and selling them to periodicals, including *The New Yorker* magazine.

After the widespread praise for *The Catcher in the Rye*, public attention drove Salinger to leave New York and move to a remote area in New England, where he became a recluse. Although he has published several short stories since the 1950s, he has never written another novel.

The Catcher in the Rye continues to speak to successive generations of teens and adolescents, and remains a perennial favorite among young readers more than 50 years after its initial publication.

88. Lord of the Flies
(1954) William Golding

William Golding's *Lord of the Flies*, a symbolic novel of schoolboys marooned on an island and their reversion to savagery, serves as a parable of the human condition. Without the structure imposed by society, Golding warned, morality would quickly dissolve, resulting in **anarchy**.

Initially, the stranded boys cooperate to build shelters and gather food. However, in the absence of civilization, order deteriorates. The youths hunt pigs, developing a taste for violence: "Kill the pig. Cut her throat. Bash her in."

Discovering that he and a companion have become prey, one boy "forgot his words, his hunger and thirst, and became fear; hopeless fear on flying feet." After a hunt for wild beasts dissolves into murder, readers discover that the "beast" is, in fact, the potential for evil within each person.

The author used **symbolism** extensively. Glasses used to build a fire signified wisdom; shattering the glasses represented the breakdown of social order. A conch shell symbolized authority; war paint applied by the boys implied rebellion against society.

The book, which inspired motion pictures in 1963 and 1990, prompted a cult-like following among youths of the post-World War II generation.

Born in 1911 near Cornwall, England, Golding followed in his father's footsteps and became a teacher. After graduating in 1935 from Oxford University, where he studied English literature, he worked in theater companies before becoming a schoolmaster.

During World War II, Golding served in the British Royal Navy. He participated in the sinking of the German battleship, *Bismarck*, and commanded a rocket-launching ship during the 1944 D-Day invasion of Normandy. After the war, he resumed teaching. His insights into boys' behavior were later reflected in *Lord of the Flies*.

A 1962 edition of *Lord of the Flies*

Lord of the Flies stemmed from Golding's horror at revelations of atrocities committed by the Nazis during World War II. "We'd found out about the human condition and it was just sheer grief at having gone through the war and to know that the war . . . hadn't settled much," he recalled in a radio interview when asked why he wrote the disturbing work.

Other works by Golding were equally dark in tone. *The Inheritors* (1955) dealt with violence involving Neanderthal Man; *Pincher Martin* (1956) featured a guilt-ridden naval officer; *Darkness Visible* (1979) recounted the trauma of a burned child during the London blitz in World War II.

Golding won the **Nobel Prize** in literature in 1983. He died in 1993.

To Kill a Mockingbird, **Harper Lee's** novel exposing racial prejudice in a southern town, helped fuel the fires of the U.S. **civil rights movement** during the 1960s.

Lee shatters her initial portrayal of a gentile southern town by revealing underlying prejudice driven by ignorance. Attorney **Atticus Finch** agrees to represent **Tom Robinson**, a black man unjustly accused of raping a white woman.

The story is revealed through the viewpoint of Finch's six-year-old daughter, **Scout**, who describes Maycomb as "a tired old town when I first knew it." Lee effectively captures the feeling of a sweltering summer in the South with phrases such as, "Men's stiff collars wilted by nine in the morning. Ladies bathed before noon . . . and by nightfall were like soft teacakes with frostings of sweat and sweet talcum."

Finch teaches his children, **Jem** and Scout, the importance of standing up against prejudice

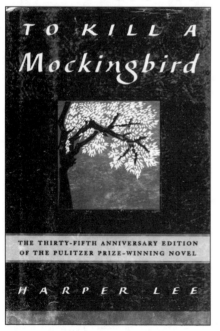

A 1995 edition of *To Kill a Mockingbird*

and ignorance. The author's message is expressed through the innocent perspective of Jem, who asks, ". . . If there's just one kind of folks, why can't they get along with each other?"

In his closing arguments, Finch asserts that white witnesses have lied, believing that their testimony will be believed solely based on the "evil assumption . . . that all Negroes lie; that all Negroes are basically immoral beings . . ."

The book's title symbolizes a loss of innocence, foretold by Finch when he cautions his offspring not to shoot a songbird: "Remember, it's a sin to kill a mockingbird."

Nelle Harper Lee was born in Monroeville, Alabama in 1926. Her father was descended from Confederate general **Robert E. Lee**. She grew up amid stories of the old South, sparking her imagination.

After college, Lee moved to New York City and began writing short stories. A literary agent encouraged her to expand one of those stories into a novel, which in 1960 became *To Kill a Mockingbird*.

Soon after its publication, the book achieved extraordinary literary success. It received a **Pulitzer Prize** in 1961, and by its second anniversary, it had sold more than five million copies. It has since been translated into 40 languages, and in 1962 became an Academy Award-winning movie starring **Gregory Peck**.

Publication rocketed Lee from obscurity to fame. She dined at the White House with President Kennedy and was appointed to the National Council of Arts by President Johnson in 1963.

In later years, Lee became a recluse. Although she published several essays and magazine articles during the 1960s, she has never written another book. Her only novel, *To Kill a Mockingbird*, remains as popular today as when it was first published.

Joseph Heller's blistering satirical novel, *Catch-22*, revealed the absurd circumstances of life among the American military during World War II.

Based on the author's experiences as an Air Force bombardier, the novel struck a chord among the American public, gaining widespread popularity by the late 1960s. The phrase "Catch-22" soon became part of the American lexicon, defined as "an illogical, unreasonable, or senseless situation."

In the book, **Captain Yossarian** is confounded by the "catch" in a military regulation when he tries to evade a combat mission by acting crazy. Regulations state that any insane individual can be grounded and relieved of hazardous duty; however, Catch-22 says that anyone who asks to be relieved from such duty because he's crazy, must really be sane—and is therefore fit to fly in combat.

Dialogue in the novel reflects Heller's wit, along with his view of war. Asked which is more important, winning the war or staying alive, Yossarian retorts, "To whom? It doesn't make a damn bit of difference who wins the war to someone who's dead. . . The enemy is anybody who's going to get you killed, no matter which side he's on."

Heller created colorful characters, raising questions over definitions of sanity and morality. Yossarian's roommate, Orr, feigns insanity in order to escape. Havermeyer, a bombardier who enjoys shooting field mice, volunteers for every mission, but refuses to take evasive action. Mess officer **Milo Minderbinder** profits off an illicit business, accepting money from the enemy.

Heller once offered this assessment of *Catch-22*: "Of course it is antiwar . . . but my intention was to make it about more than that—about the government, about society, and about how things were at the time, in 1961-62. I've been lucky in that most of the

A 1961 edition of *Catch-22*

things I wrote about . . . have not improved since then, so the book seems to have remained relevant."

Joseph Heller was born in Brooklyn, New York in 1923. During World War II, Heller flew 60 missions in Europe, an experience that deeply affected his outlook on life.

Catch-22 initially received mixed reviews, won no prizes, and made no best-seller lists. However, it gained greater acceptance among readers over time; by the end of the 1960s, with the Vietnam war at its height, the book had become a classic.

Other novels by Heller include *Something Happened* (1974), *Good as Gold* (1979), and *Closing Time* (1994), a sequel to *Catch-22*.

None of his later works achieved the popularity of *Catch-22*, the antiwar novel that captured the sentiments and imagination of a generation.

91. Silent Spring
(1962) Rachel Carson

Rachel Carson's 1962 best-seller, *Silent Spring*, launched the **environmental movement**, issuing a dire warning about the dangers of **pesticides**.

"Every human being is now subjected to contact with dangerous chemicals, from the moment of conception until death," Carson wrote.

Carson was born on a farm in Springdale, Pennsylvania in 1907. After receiving a masters degree in marine biology from Johns Hopkins University, she taught zoology and later became an editor of publications for the U.S. Fish & Wildlife Service.

Rachel Carson

Carson gained fame as a conservationist in 1951 with publication of *The Sea Around Us*, part of a trilogy of books she wrote about the ecology of the sea.

After spraying of **DDT** killed birds in a friend's wildlife sanctuary, Carson questioned the impact of pesticides on the chain of life. Concerned over the rampant increase in pesticide usage following World War II, she wrote *Silent Spring*, alerting the public to the dark side of science posed by synthetic chemicals. The *New York Times* published book excerpts,

and CBS News presented a televised special based on Carson's work.

Carson weathered a storm of criticism, including scathing attacks on her credibility from chemical companies. However, her deep scientific insight, combined with her descriptive writing style, enabled *Silent Spirng* to reach a wide audience newly interested in its message of conservation. Her concerns led to Congressional hearings over the impact of pesticides on the environment and human health, and resulted in eventual tougher government controls over these chemicals.

Ironically, while writing *Silent Spring*, Carson was diagnosed with breast cancer—a disease scientists now realize can be caused by exposure to toxic chemicals. Despite surgery and radiation treatment, she died in 1964.

Although Carson did not live long enough to witness the progress generated by her book, environmentalists give her great credit for her efforts. Vice President Al Gore, who authored a popular environmental book himself, has said that *Silent Spring* "changed the course of history."

The book led to increasing public awareness of environmental issues, spurring creation of the **Environmental Protection Agency** and declaration of Earth Day in 1970. Within two years, the Clean Air Act and Clean Water Act also became law. After the pesticide DDT was banned in 1972, several endangered bird species, including eagles, were saved from extinction.

Although many advances in environmental protection resulted from Carson's work, ironically, total production of pesticides in the United States has increased by 400 percent since *Silent Spring* appeared.

The concerns raised by Rachel Carson over the balance of nature and survival of mankind in a world tainted by toxic chemicals remain tragically relevant, four decades after the publication of *Silent Spring*.

92. The Feminine Mystique
(1963)   Betty Friedan

Betty Friedan's *The Feminine Mystique* shattered the myth that all women could find total fulfillment as wives and mothers. The book raised women's consciences, provoked a storm of controversy, and helped launch the **feminist movement** of the latter part of the 20th century.

"I married, had children, lived according to the feminine mystique as a suburban house-wife," wrote Friedan, who likened the condition of housewives to slavery. "They are in a trap," she declared.

Friedan criticized women's passive roles, and the stereotype of females as weak and dependent upon men. Women should aspire to attain psychological independence and economic freedom, argued Friedan, who believed women deserved full equality with men, at home and in the workplace.

In her book, she described the life of a typical American wife and mother as a child-centered lonely existence. It was filled with the boring routine of housework, hidden behind the romantic myth of domestic happiness for which most women sacrificed any opportunity for personal fulfillment. Friedan called this idealization of the role of women, "**the feminine mystique**," a conspiracy to deprive women of the chance to compete equally with men.

Friedan's descriptions struck a chord with many women. Her book launched the feminist movement of the 1960s and 70s, and encouraged more women to seek jobs and pursue careers. It also spurred legislative reforms to end sex discrimination in the workplace and narrow wage gaps between men and women.

The author was born **Naomi Goldstein** in Peoria, Illinois in 1921. While working as a reporter for a labor publication in 1947, she married Carl Friedman, an actor who later dropped the "m" from his name. At the same time, she began publishing pamphlets sup-

Betty Friedan

porting women's rights, arguing that women should receive equal pay for equal work.

While pregnant with her second child, Friedan was fired for requesting maternity leave again. She became a full-time wife and mother in a suburban neighborhood, but soon felt dissatisfied and missed her career. After polling former female college classmates who were also housewives, Friedan realized that others shared her feelings.

Friedan spent five years writing her book while her children were at school. When it was published, it was an immediate success. Within three years, *The Feminine Mystique* had sold more than three million copies.

Friedan became a founder of the **National Organization for Women** (NOW) in 1966, and served as its first president until 1970. She is considered by many to be the "mother" of the modern women's movement, and *The Feminine Mystique* is viewed as one of the most influential books on the role and status of women in American society in the 20th century.

"The medium is the message," **Marshall McLuhan** declared in *Understanding Media: The Extensions of Man*. Published in 1964, the book challenged old assumptions about, and predicted new trends in, **mass communication**.

McLuhan was among the first to perceive the power of the emerging mass media, which was then limited to television and radio. Conventional wisdom held that the content of a message was more important than its form. McLuhan, by contrast, argued that the method of communication could have a dramatic impact in its own right. A story took on new meanings when viewed on television or heard on radio instead of read in print, he believed.

A 1964 edition of *Understanding Media*

Decades before development of the **Internet**, McLuhan foresaw that **electronic communication** would forever change perceptions, effectively making the world smaller by linking people around the globe through tech-nology. "We shape our tools," he announced, "and afterwards our tools shape us."

McLuhan viewed electronic communication as an extension of the human nervous system. Images viewed on television are reflections of ourselves, he explained. McLuhan also coined the term "**global village**" long before the phrase became political-ly popular.

In his book, he predicted, "Rapidly, we approach the final phase of the extensions of man—the technological simulation of con-sciousness, when the creative process of know-ing will be collectively and corporately extend-ed to the whole of human society. . ."

Hailed as a technology prophet, McLuhan enjoyed an initial cult-like following. The rise of the Internet in the 1990s led to a resur-gence in popularity of his views.

Born in 1911 in Edmonton, Canada, McLuhan studied English literature at the University of Manitoba and obtained a Ph.D. from Cambridge University. After holding sev-eral teaching posts, he was appointed director of the University of Toronto's Centre for Culture and Technology in 1963.

In 1962, he wrote *The Gutenberg Galaxy: The Making of Technological Man*, in which he assessed the impact of literacy—made possible by invention of the Gutenberg printing press—on civilization. Foreseeing that the mass media's impact would be equally substan-tial in revolutionizing the world, he published *Understanding Media*. His later works, *War and Peace in the Global Village*, and *Laws of Media: The New Science* also addressed the evolution of a high-tech world.

McLuhan's reputation as a technology guru grew. He accumulated honorary degrees from a half dozen universities, became popular as a speaker, and received many awards. Many col-leges and universities in Canada and the United States now offer courses on his work.

94. Unsafe at Any Speed
(1965) Ralph Nader

Unsafe at Any Speed, **consumer advocate Ralph Nader's** exposé of the dangers posed by unsafe American automobiles, led to passage of the 1966 **National Traffic and Motor Vehicle Safety Act**, and launched the modern consumer protection movement.

In the book, Nader blamed car manufacturers for deaths caused by poor automobile designs. He accused the U.S. **automobile industry** of choosing profits over expenditures for safety. Ford, Chrysler, American Motors, and General Motors failed to use existing technology to improve safety, Nader argued. He faulted the automobile industry for placing more emphasis on sporty appearances than on safety.

Nader's book revealed that one model, the **Chevrolet Corvair**, had caused more deaths than any other car. The Corvair was so unstable that even a small bump in the road could cause it to spin or roll over, Nader charged. The book stated that despite having knowledge of such accidents, General Motors pocketed $1.7 billion in profits in 1964, yet spent only a small fraction of that sum—$1 million—on safety research.

Nader believed that consumers should have the right to know about a vehicle's safety record. Moreover, manufacturers should have an obligation to produce safe cars. He argued that "the true mark of a humane society must be what it does about prevention of accident injuries, not the cleaning up of them afterward."

The book drew widespread attention following its publication in 1965. The *New York Times* ran excerpts on its front page; the book quickly became a bestseller and eventually sold more than a half million copies.

Born in Winsted, Connecticut in 1934, Nader attended Princeton University, and graduated from Harvard Law School; in 1964, he became a consultant to the U.S. Department of Labor.

Ralph Nader

Concerned over the accident statistics he came across in his legal work, Nader wrote *Unsafe at Any Speed*, sparking U.S. Senate hearings on automobile safety. For tackling General Motors, America's largest corporation at the time, he was compared to David attacking Goliath.

Nader became the target of private investigators hired by General Motors to discredit him during the Senate hearings. The tactic was exposed, leading to outrage over the company's attempt to intimidate a federal witness. In 1966, Congress enacted unprecedented legislation to regulate the powerful auto industry.

Soon, Nader called for strict government regulations in other areas. His team of consumer activists, dubbed "**Nader's Raiders**," have conducted many safety studies and helped launch numerous reforms in areas such as workplace safety, health care practices, and the environment.

Unsafe at Any Speed is the book that virtually began consumer advocacy in America, and it has helped prevent countless injuries and deaths from auto accidents.

Quotations of Chairman Mao
(1966) Mao Tse-tung

Quotations of Chairman Mao, also known as *Mao's Little Red Book*, shaped the thinking of a generation of Chinese people and became one of the most intensely studied books in the world.

A peasant born in 1893 in China's Hunan province, **Mao Tse-tung** co-founded the **Chinese Communist party** and led the revolution that took control of China in 1949. He founded the **People's Republic of China**, and became leader of the new nation.

Mao ordered redistribution of lands, elimination of landlords in rural areas, and rapid industrialization of urban areas. His **Great Leap Forward** program failed, at a cost of millions of lives.

Quotations of Chairman Mao was published in 1966 as a guidebook for the **Cultural Revolution**, an ideological movement to sway the thinking of the masses. The book, containing Mao's **political philosophies**, became required reading for all Chinese people.

Study groups met to discuss the quotations and find applications to their daily lives. Mao's word was treated as absolute authority in China. In the West, revolutionary and pseudo-revolutionary groups found it fashionable to carry copies of Mao's work and quote from it.

In his book, Mao criticized Western thought and viewed the United States as China's greatest enemy. He referred to Hitler and the Russian czar as "paper tigers" who were ultimately overthrown, but reserved his harshest attacks for America.

"U.S. imperialism has not yet been overthrown and it has the atom bomb. I believe it also will be overthrown. It, too, is a paper tiger."

Although Mao had earlier encouraged an open exchange of ideas, during the Cultural Revolution he ordered a crackdown on free thinking. Mao mobilized students as "Red Guards" and taught young people to denounce those in authority. To justify "re-education" sessions, he urged exposure of those people he viewed as subversive.

"We still have to wage a protracted struggle against bourgeois and petty-bourgeois ideology . . . All erroneous ideas, all poisonous weeds . . . must be subjected to criticism."

People were imprisoned for harboring "incorrect" thoughts. Millions died; many more lost their jobs or educational opportunities and were forced to work on collective farms. Ultimately, the Cultural Revolution failed at a terrible cost.

Mao's views changed when Chinese relations with the Soviet Union became strained. In 1972, he met with President Richard Nixon to foster closer relations with the United States.

The Chinese Communist party declared an end to the Cultural Revolution after Mao's death in 1976. In the 1980s, Mao's views were officially denounced.

By the end of the 20th century, Chinese leaders acknowledged Mao's accomplishments as the founder of modern China, while also recognizing the tragedies resulting from his leadership.

Mao Tse-tung

When it was published in 1967, **Gabriel García Márquez's** *One Hundred Years of Solitude* was hailed by The *New York Times* as "the first piece of literature since the Book of Genesis that should be required reading for the entire human race."

The book that inspired such high praise relates the rise and fall of **Macondo**, a fictitious South American village founded by **José Arcadio Buendía** and populated by several generations of his descendants. Using a blend of autobiographical material, folk tales, and stories inspired by the author's ancestors, the village Márquez created has come to be viewed as symbolic of all underdeveloped **Latin American countries**.

A master of **magical realism**, Márquez weaves real and miraculous elements in describing events that transpire in the enchanted town.

"Many years later, as he faced the firing squad, Colonel Aureliano Buendía was to remember that distant afternoon when his father took him to discover ice," begins the novel. Later, the story matter-of-factly relates fantastic occurrences, such as a town overcome by amnesia and characters who communicate with spirits.

For example, after Ursula Buendía discovers that the ghost of a murdered man seeks water to clean his wound, "from then on she placed water jugs all about the house." In each generation, characters repeat the mistakes and passions of their ancestors. Over the years, descendants of Buendía endure civil war and shattered dreams. Despite being surrounded by a village filled with people, however, each must in the end come to terms with solitude.

Márquez was born in Aracataca, a Colombian banana town founded by his grandfather. Tragedy marked the year of his birth in 1928, when government troops massacred hundreds of striking banana workers.

Márquez later evoked the event in *One Hundred Years of Solitude*.

While attending the university in Bogotá, he became a reporter for a newspaper, which printed his first short story. After rioting forced closure of the university, Márquez studied law in Cartagena, but dropped out to pursue a literary career.

While writing *One Hundred Years of Solitude*, Márquez sold his car and pawned household appliances to support his family. Sensing the importance of his work, the entire community began helping out, offering credit and forgiving his debts. Márquez included himself, his wife, and his friends in the novel.

One Hundred Years of Solitude, won four international prizes and brought Márquez worldwide fame. His other novels include *No One Writes to the Colonel* (1968), *The Autumn of the Patriarch* (1976), and *The General in His Labyrinth* (1990). In 1982, the author received the **Nobel Prize** in literature for his work.

A 1991 edition of Márquez's book

Bury My Heart at Wounded Knee
(1971)   Dee Brown

Bury My Heart at Wounded Knee, **Dee Brown**'s moving account of the systematic destruction of **native American** life during the late 19th century, changed America's view of the past and drew attention to the treatment of native Americans.

The book was the first to present history of the West from a native American viewpoint, sympathetically portraying Indians' bravery and suffering at the hands of white settlers and the American government. Opening with the **Long Walk** of the Navajos in 1860, the book described the bloody **Plains Wars** of the late 1800s, and exposed the **genocide** and **displacement** of native Americans by the U.S. government.

The author cited government documents to demonstrate racist views held by members of the U.S. military and Congress. He dispelled the euphemistic term, "Manifest Destiny" used to justify forcing native people off of their lands and onto reservations in order to make room for white settlers; those who resisted were systematically starved or killed.

The books ends with the

1979 edition of *Bury My Heart at Wounded Knee*

massacre of Sioux men, women, and children at **Wounded Knee** in **South Dakota**. Brown juxtaposed religious symbolism against the massacre's tragic aftermath in the book's final passage:

"When the first torn and bleeding bodies were carried into the candlelit church, those who were conscious could see Christmas greenery hanging from the open rafters . . . above the pulpit was strung a crudely lettered banner: PEACE ON EARTH, GOODWILL TO MEN."

Until publication of *Bury My Heart at Wounded Knee*, the history of the American West had been written by its conquerors. Native Americans had mostly been portrayed as bloodthirsty savages. Brown sympathetically depicted native American leaders as courageous and reasonable, while exposing the suffering of their people.

A trip to Indian regions led Brown to write *Bury My Heart at Wounded Knee*. A meticulous researcher, he included eyewitness accounts and interviews chronicling genocide by the U.S. Cavalry. When the book was published, it elicited shock, then shame, among many readers. Called "shattering" by the *Washington Post*, it has sold more than five million copies and been translated into 17 languages.

Two years after the book's publication, members of the **American Indian Movement** seized the town of Wounded Knee to protest reservation conditions, drawing public attention to the present-day treatment of Indians.

The author was born D. Alexander Brown in a Louisiana logging town in 1908, and grew up hearing stories of the Old West from his grandmother.

Brown has authored more than two dozen books, including historical novels and nonfiction. His works, especially *Bury My Heart at Wounded Knee*, have forever changed public perception of how the American West was settled.

98. The Gulag Archipelago
(1973-1975)   Aleksandr Solzhenitsyn

The Gulag Archipelago, **Aleksandr Solzhenitsyn's** searing exposé of the brutal **Soviet Communist penal system**, is both a literary triumph and an important historical document.

Imprisoned in a labor camp, Solzhenitsyn spent eight years memorizing names, records, and oral accounts of other prisoners. Determined to tell the world about the *gulag* system of camps, Solzhenitsyn documented his experiences—and those of other prisoners—after his 1953 release.

His first exposé of life in a Soviet prison camp came with publication of "One Day in the Life of Ivan Denisovich" in 1962. The short story created an international sensation—and caused the Soviet government to ban publication of Solzhenitsyn's works.

He circulated his next books illegally, publishing them abroad. After the KGB—the Soviet secret police—seized his manuscript of *The Gulag Archipelago*, Solzhenitsyn smuggled a copy to Paris, where volume one was published in 1973. The work, along with subsequent volumes, exposed records of the *gulag*, which expanded dramatically under **Josef Stalin's** rule. From 1928 to 1953, 40 to 50 million prisoners were confined in the camps, according to Solzhenitsyn; 15 to 30 million died.

Within the novel, Solzhenitsyn explored the human condition: "It was granted to me to carry away from my prison years on my bent back . . . this essential experience: how a human being becomes evil and how good."

Within each human heart, he wrote, there exists potential for goodness and evil. "It is impossible to expel evil from the world in its entirety, but it is possible to constrict it within each person," he concluded.

Born into a family of Cossack intellectuals in 1918, Solzhenitsyn served in the Soviet army during World War II. As commander of an artillery battery at the front, he earned medals and was promoted to captain.

Near the end of the war, Solzhenitsyn sent a letter to a friend in which he criticized Soviet ruler Stalin's leadership. As a result, Solzhenitsyn was arrested and imprisoned for eight years. He endured back-breaking work, brutality, starvation, and a bout with cancer.

Awarded the **Nobel Prize** in literature in 1970, Solzhenitsyn declined to travel to Sweden to accept it for fear he would not be allowed to return home. Convicted of treason, Solzhenitsyn was exiled in 1974. After collecting his Nobel Prize, he moved to the United States. In 1974 and 1975, he published volumes two and three of *The Gulag Archipelago.*

His works remained forbidden in the Soviet Union until a policy of **glasnost** (openness) was adopted during the 1980s. After the Soviet Union collapsed in 1990 his citizenship was restored; he returned to Russia in 1994.

A 1973 edition of *The Gulag Archipelago*

99. Beloved

(1987) Toni Morrison

Beloved, **Toni Morrison's** highly-acclaimed novel, combines lyrical prose in the African-American storytelling tradition, with elements of **magical realism** to address issues of **black culture, history,** and **identity**.

The novel tells the story of **Sethe**, an escaped slave haunted by the ghost of her dead child, **Beloved**. In the book, characters accept the spirit as a fact of life, although its identity is not at first known. Sethe's mother-in-law comments, "Not a house in the country ain't packed to its rafters with some dead Negro's grief. We lucky this ghost is a baby."

The baby ghost has a penchant for mischief, leaving fingerprints in cake icing. Sethe, now a mother living in freedom, must come to terms with the realization that the ghost is that of her own murdered child.

Pursued by a runaway slave hunter during an escape attempt many years earlier, Sethe slit her infant daughter's throat rather than allow her to be captured and raised in slavery.

Set in Ohio in 1873, the novel, through flashback, reveals the horrors of slavery. For example, Morrison describes the bit, a cruel device placed in the mouth to punish a rebellious slave. Sethe recalls her mistreatment as a slave and the humiliation of knowing that her husband, hidden in a loft, was " . . . looking and letting it happen . . . And if he was that broken then, then he is also and certainly dead now."

The past also impacts **Denver**, Sethe's troubled teenage daughter, so isolated that she communicates only with her mother and the ghost of her dead sister.

When Sethe's terrible secret is revealed, she confronts the horror of her past, then puts the past behind her. Readers must ponder the meaning of love—and whether desire to protect one's children at all cost can justify a seemingly unconscionable act. The novel conveys a message of healing aimed at the African-American community: it is time to let go of the past, however painful, and move on.

Born **Chloe Anthony Wofford** in Lorain, Ohio in 1931, Morrison grew up in a poor family with four children. After graduating from Howard University, she obtained a Master's degree in English from Cornell University. In 1958, she married Harold Morrison, a Jamaican architect, but they later divorced.

Morrison published her first novel in 1970. After a series of critically acclaimed books in the 1970s and 80s, *Beloved*, which won the 1988 **Pulitzer Prize** for fiction, brought Morrison international fame. In 1993, she became the first African-American woman to receive the **Nobel Prize** in literature.

Toni Morrison

How was the universe formed? Where did we come from? Will the universe someday end?

Stephen Hawking, one of the world's most brilliant physicists, addressed these and other questions in his 1988 bestseller, *A Brief History of Time*. Divining answers would be a triumph in human reason, Hawking asserted, "for then we would know the mind of God."

During the next decade, technological advances led to scientific verification of many predictions Hawking made in his book. In 1998, on the tenth anniversary of his classic work, Hawking released an updated edition with a new chapter on **wormholes** and **space-time travel**, proofs of earlier theories, and numerous illustrations—including photographs taken by the Hubble space telescope.

In a forward to the new edition, Hawking notes that Einstein's **Theory of Relativity** suggests that mankind might create wormholes, tubes connecting different regions of space-time. "If so, we might be able to use them for rapid travel around the galaxy or travel back in time," he theorizes.

Hawking also discusses new findings by the **Cosmic Background Explorer** satellite. It has measured time back to within 300,000 years of the universe's creation, revealing "wrinkles" in space-time fabric foreseen by Hawking. Within a few years, he predicts, we will know if "we live in a universe that is completely self-contained and without beginning or end."

The new edition, like his earlier work, uses clear language to explain complex scientific principles to the general public. Hawking's work has also influenced scientists worldwide.

Born in Oxfordshire, England in 1942, Hawking studied mathematics and physics at Oxford and Cambridge universities. Despite suffering from a degenerative neuromuscular disease, amyotrophic lateral sclerosis, he obtained a Ph.D. in physics. The disease later confined him to a wheelchair, but never slowed his quest for knowledge.

Hawking amassed a reputation as a scientific genius for applying quantum physics and relativity laws to develop the "**Big Bang**" concept of an expanding universe, as well as theorizing about the properties of **black holes**.

In 1974, Hawking became one of the youngest fellows elected by England's Royal Society. During the 1970s, he also became professor of gravitational physics at Cambridge. In 1979, he was appointed to the Cambridge Lucasian professorship of mathematics, a position once held by Sir **Isaac Newton**.

Hawking has also written *The Large Scale Structure of Space-Time* (1973), *Superspace and Supergravity* (1981), and *The Very Early Universe* (1983).

A Brief History in Time has sold over nine million copies in 40 languages worldwide. The updated edition once again makes cutting-edge scientific discoveries accessible to a global audience without expertise in the scientific field.

Stephen Hawking

Trivia Quiz & Projects

Test your knowledge and challenge your friends with the following questions. The answers are contained in the entries noted.

1. Which ancient Greek epic poem tells the tragic story of the Trojan War? (see no. 3)
2. What ancient Roman treatise on government did America's founding fathers use as an inspiration when they created the Declaration of Independence? (see no.10)
3. Which Japanese tale is considered by many historians to be the world's first novel? (see no.12)
4. When did a Polish astronomer publish his controversial and radical theory about the Earth's relationship to the sun? (see no. 20)
5. Why is a 17th century English writer and philosopher given credit for sparking both the American and the French Revolutions? (see no. 26)
6. Which 18th century English writer called for full civil and political rights for women in one of the world's earliest feminist documents? (see no. 33)
7. Which escaped slave's autobiography made him a powerful voice in the abolitionist movement to outlaw slavery? (see no. 40)
8. What classic novel described the ordeals suffered by poor children as well as the dismal social conditions of mid-19th century England? (see no. 43)
9. Where did the author of the controversial theory of evolution make his historic scientific discoveries? (see no. 47)
10. Which 19th century classic adventure novel is said to be the originator of all modern American literature? (see no. 54)
11. Why was a well-known English author forced to revive his famous literary creation after he had killed him off? (see no. 56)
12. How did a blind, deaf, and mute young woman overcome her handicaps to become a crusader for the world's underprivileged and disadvantaged people? (see no. 61)
13. When do all the events take place in the novel that many critics consider the greatest literary work of the 20th century? (see no. 69)
14. Who is credited with having virtually created the genre of hard-boiled detective fiction with his classic 1930 novel? (see no. 76)
15. Which novel's title has entered the American lexicon as a phrase meaning an "illogical, unreasonable, or senseless situation?" (see no. 90)
16. Who helped create the American environmental movement with her groundbreaking book describing the dangerous use of pesticides? (see no. 91)

Suggested Projects

1. Choose a book you have read which you consider worthy enough to be included on a list of 100 greatest books. Write a brief essay describing either the book's plot (fiction) or subject matter (nonfiction), as well as the reasons why you feel it should be included on such a list. In addition, write a paragraph or two about the author of the work.

2. Choose a time period in history during which any of the works listed in this book was written. Do some research and describe three or four other major events that occurred during this period. Then decide whether or not you believe any of the other events you described had an influence on the author and the creation of his or her book. Write a paragraph or two explaining the reasons why.

Index

Index

Index

Index